What a *Great* *Word*

FOR GRADS

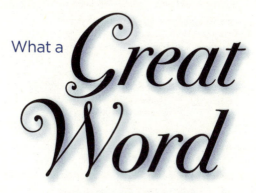

A DEVOTIONAL

KAREN MOORE

Faith *Words*

NEW YORK   NASHVILLE

FaithWords
Hachette Book Group
1290 Avenue of the Americas, New York, NY 10104
faithwords.com
twitter.com/faithwords

First Edition: April 2019

FaithWords is a division of Hachette Book Group, Inc. The FaithWords name and logo are trademarks of Hachette Book Group, Inc.

The publisher is not responsible for websites (or their content) that are not owned by the publisher.

The Hachette Speakers Bureau provides a wide range of authors for speaking events. To find out more, go to www.hachettespeakersbureau.com or call (866) 376-6591.

ISBNs: 978-1-5460-3561-9 (paper over board), 978-1-5460-3562-6 (ebook)

Printed in the United States of America

LSC-C

10 9 8 7 6 5 4 3 2 1

Contents

THE PRAYER OF SAINT PATRICK

GOD'S PROMISES

129

Congratulations, Graduate!

You've just completed one important phase of your education. Now you're on to lifelong learning, where you're sure to be inspired and challenged more than you've ever been before. As you step into the world, you'll be continually discovering new things. Your life outside formal education still requires thought and study, and an attitude that you can do it... whatever "it" is for you!

This little book is designed to inspire your thoughts as you think about the ways that you hope to move forward from here. Each word is genuinely directed toward aligning your work, your spiritual growth, and your hopes and dreams as you are molded and shaped into the person God intends you to be.

It might help to create a journal built around the forty words you see here and then notice how your perceptions of these special words change with time and experience. As you focus on each word, make it personal to you. Let it motivate your heart and inspire your spirit.

There's a big world out there, and you will need the full armor of God to face it each day. No worries! He knows you, sees you, and is ready to walk with you from this day forward.

It's exciting to see what you will choose to become both personally and in your lifework, so that you make a difference to those around you.

Blessings and joy to you on your graduation! Now go celebrate your first great milestone!

In His Love,
Karen Moore

Attitude

The longer I live the more I realize
the impact of attitude on life.
Attitude to me is more important than the past,
than education, than money, than circumstances,
than failures, than success,
than what others think, or say, or do.
I am convinced that life is 10% what happens to me
and 90% how I react to it.

Chuck Swindoll

Serve

Hats Off to You!

*"As for me and my family, we will **serve** the Lord."*

Joshua 24:15 NCV

Graduation caps, those square black boards with tassels, are a symbol of accomplishment. They may not fit your head the way you would like, but they fit the occasion and serve to celebrate all you've accomplished.

After the ceremony becomes a sweet memory and you're finished with the celebrations, your new life will begin, and everything may change. You'll probably wear a lot of other hats. Some of those won't fit you well either, but you'll try them on just to see if they might work out. One hat may take you on to get more education; another might send you off to work or into the military. Whatever hat you choose will guide the steps you take from then on.

Looking back at your square graduation cap, you might consider it as square number one, the one that jump-starts your life and opens new doors. It's a square that is just one piece in the mosaic of the person you will become, but it will be one you return to often as you recall what you've learned.

As you venture into the four corners of the world, keep in mind the things that are most relevant to you. Perhaps one corner of your life is education, adventure, discovering new ideas and places; another corner is family and friends. You may see a third corner as simply becoming the real you. The fourth corner is your foundation stone, your life in Christ, and it asks you to recognize the One who holds you squarely in His hand, the One who will never let go of you no matter what other corners you choose to go around.

What hat will you wear in your faith? The world will ask you to stand up for what you believe. Israel's leader, Joshua, asked the people of his day to make a choice about whom they would serve. He said, "If you don't want to serve the Lord, you must choose for yourselves today whom you will serve" (Joshua 24:15 NCV). Basically, he told them, you can serve the world, or you can serve God.

May you choose wisely, and may your choice bring you the same kind of joy as tossing your hat into the air on Graduation Day. Blessings to you!

KEEP LEARNING

The head grows by taking in, but the heart grows by giving out.

Author unknown

YOUR CALLING

God doesn't call the equipped, He equips the called.

Author unknown

SERVANT LEADERS

But Jesus called them together and said, "You know that the rulers in this world lord it over their people, and officials flaunt their authority over those under them. But among you it will be different. Whoever wants to be a leader among you must be your servant, and whoever wants to be first among you must become your slave." Matthew 20:25–27 NLT

ABILITY LEVELS

The Lord doesn't ask about your ability, only your availability; and if you prove your dependability, the Lord will increase your capability! Author unknown

WHO YOU ARE

We are not built for ourselves, but for God.
Not for service for God, but for God! Oswald Chambers

WHEN YOU LOOK BACK

You will find, as you look back on your life, that the moments that stand out are the moments when you have done things for others.

Henry Drummond

YOU'RE IMPORTANT

They might not need me; but they might.
I'll let my head be just in sight;
A smile as small as mine might be
Precisely their necessity.

Emily Dickinson

THE WAY TO HAPPINESS

I don't know what your destiny will be, but one thing I know. The only ones of you who will be really happy, are those who have sought and found how to serve.

Albert Schweitzer

Prayer

Lord, grant me a servant heart; the kind that is willing to stand up for what I believe, to share what I learn, and that aspires to serve You in all that I do. As I go forward from this day, remind me that You are always with me. Help me to make honest efforts as I go into the world and do my best to treat everyone fairly and with dignity.

Lord, as I stand on square one, remind me of all I've learned so that I am inspired to make wise choices. Bless each step that I take from here and go before me to the places I will go next. Thank You for helping me to grow and for giving me such an amazing start.

Amen

Attitude

An "All Things Are Possible" Attitude

Finally, all of you should be of one mind. Sympathize with each other. Love each other as brothers and sisters. Be tenderhearted, and keep a humble attitude.   1 Peter 3:8 NLT

What kind of attitude will best serve you as you step into your future? Do you need to be bold and fearless, ready to take on things that are already bigger and stronger than you are?

Maybe you need a positive attitude that pumps you up so that everything in front of you looks possible and causes you to feel excited as you keep moving forward. How you think about each step you take makes a difference that helps or hinders your progress.

Take a moment and imagine the word "impossible." Now break it into two words with a little tweak, so it becomes, "I'm possible!" With you in the picture, things can change. With God's help, the One through whom all things are possible, you've suddenly become a force to be reckoned with. It's a question of attitude!

Where do you want to go? How much do you hope to achieve? Whatever it is, if you put all your ideas and opportunities into God's hands, He will help you accomplish your goals.

Norman Vincent Peale was a big possibility thinker. He said that it's always good to "become a possibilitarian. No matter how dark things seem to be or actually are, raise your sights and see possibilities—always see them, for they are always there."

With that kind of positive, strong, intentional, and persistent attitude, you're sure to accomplish incredible things.

One more thing: Remember that you have a lot going for you as you take on the world, and the more you adopt an attitude of prayer, the more you'll see God's hand at work in all you want to do. So get ready! Get set! Go! The world is waiting for you!

STAND BACK, PLEASE!

The world stands aside to let people pass who know where they are going.   Author unknown

DEFINE SIGNIFICANCE

If you think you're too insignificant to have an impact, try going to bed with a mosquito in your bedroom.   Anita Roddick

GETTING THE RIGHT PERSPECTIVE

Two prisoners looked out between iron bars,
One saw the mud; the other saw stars.   Author unknown

A NEW ATTITUDE

You were taught, with regard to your former way of life, to put off your old self, which is being corrupted by its deceitful desires; to be made new in the attitude of your minds; and to put on the new self, created to be like God in true righteousness and holiness.

Ephesians 4:22–24 NIV

COLORFUL THOUGHTS

Attitude is the paintbrush of the mind. It can color any situation.

Author unknown

YOUR FREEDOM

The last of the human freedoms is to choose one's attitude in any given set of circumstances.   Viktor Frankl

CHOOSE YOUR KIND OF DAY

Today, I can choose to complain because it's raining,
Or rejoice that the grass is getting watered for free.
Today, I can blame my parents for what they didn't do,
Or thank God for all that they did do.

Today, I can grieve that old friends move away,
Or be happy that new friends come along.
Today, I can complain that I have to go to school,
Or I can be happy that I have a chance to learn new things.
Today, I am the sculptor of my day, ready to shape all that can be.
Today I will choose what kind of day I will have.   Author unknown

Prayer

Lord, please help me to look to You for all that I do. When I am not certain of my direction, grant me a positive and caring attitude toward others and toward the goals I pursue. Encourage my efforts by guiding me through Your Word and by putting people in my life who can inspire my thoughts and actions. Please remind me that I can always come back to You when my attitude needs a major adjustment. I thank You, Lord, for the things you do to shape my heart and mind.   Amen

Change

Changing into Amazing You

*Do the things that show you really have **changed** your hearts and lives. And don't think you can say to yourselves, "Abraham is our father." I tell you that God could make children for Abraham from these rocks.*

Matthew 3:8–9 NCV

The one thing you can be certain will follow your Graduation Day will be change. Sometimes you'll invite change into your life; other times it will simply carry you along to discover something new. You may have already opted for a new job or to live in a different city. That means you have to be willing to explore what that job or city may offer that could change your view of the world. You may have decided to further your education, so you can move into a field of study that is entirely different than anything you have pursued before. These changes can be exciting. They can stimulate your growth and motivate your heart and mind. They can also be somewhat daunting.

The world at large will beckon you to change. It will invite you to try on new philosophies, explore the infinite avenues of social media, and even challenge your faith. Trying on new ideas is healthy and learning about the latest trends in pop culture may also serve you well. Keep in mind, though, that the One who never changes, Your Father in Heaven, will also be near you. Seek Him with your whole heart, not because you grew up going to church, and not because your parents believe in Him, but because you know you are His child.

Your opinions will continue to alter with each exploration; your learning curve will be modified and intensified and go on for a lifetime, and the world will continue to beckon you. Change is beautiful when it guides you and strengthens you and causes you to grow in wonderful ways. Hold fast to your foundation of faith as you go because your unchanging Father in Heaven will keep His grip on you.

YOUR PERSONAL SERENITY PRAYER

God grant me the serenity to accept the people I cannot change, the courage to change the one I can, and the wisdom to know that it's me.

Author unknown

DON'T GET TOO COMFORTABLE

If you would attain to what you are not yet, you must always be displeased by what you are. For where you are pleased with yourself, there you have remained. Keep adding, keep walking, and keep advancing.

Saint Augustine

CHANGE YOUR THINKING

And he said: "Truly I tell you, unless you change and become like little children, you will never enter the kingdom of heaven."

Matthew 18:3 NIV

BE THE CHANGE

Be the change you want to see in the world.   Mahatma Gandhi

BE THE BLESSING

God might say, "Be the blessing you want to see in the world." Bless those around you by what you stand for, what you believe, and what you do. Be the blessing.

K. Moore

CHANGE DIRECTION

A bend in the road is not the end of the road, unless you fail to make the turn.

Author unknown

HUMBLE CHANGE

Lord, when we are wrong, make us willing to change. And when we are right, make us easy to live with.

Peter Marshall

Prayer

Dear Lord, I feel somewhat overwhelmed, flooded by all the change that is up ahead. I don't want to navigate those changes without You. Please be my anchor and my guide so that I don't get carried away, or float down the wrong stream. Help me to adapt to my new direction and go with the flow, trusting You to be there with me. I pray that I will embrace every change with a positive spirit. I am so grateful for the opportunities in front of me. I pray to stay strong and steady as I go, safe, in Your care and keeping. Amen

Choices

Daily Decisions and Constant Choices

*Wise **choices** will watch over you. Understanding will keep you safe.*

Proverbs 2:11 NLT

One of life's awesome challenges is to be faced with choices, decisions, selecting one way over another. Sure, some choices don't take any time. You know what you like, and you know enough about yourself that you can figure out when something won't work well for you. You have experience with making the right decisions.

As you move out into the world, though, you'll be faced with new decisions, new perspectives, and new ways of thinking. Those new things will require you to choose what you want to do about them. Sometimes you'll be right and wise and grateful for the choices you made. Other times, you'll wonder what you were thinking and how you got yourself into the mess that followed a poor choice you made.

The thing to remember is that even when you make a bad decision, you are free to take it to God in prayer and seek guidance and direction to get back on the right path. You can choose again. Erich Fromm wrote, "Our capacity to choose changes constantly with our practice of life. The longer we continue to make the wrong decisions, the more our heart hardens; the more often we make the right decisions, the more our heart softens or, better perhaps, comes alive."

Our current culture often sees nothing as truly right or wrong. Chances are you already have some experience that tells you that isn't the case. There are clear right and wrong answers. You will always have to choose, but your heart and the Holy Spirit will guide your decisions. Your best choices will cause you to "come alive" with great joy.

Go confidently, then, because you know you are not alone. With God's help, you will make good decisions and great choices, and you will find amazing opportunities ahead of you.

CONSIDERING CHOICES

In any moment of decision, the best thing you can do is the right thing. The next best thing is the wrong thing. The worst thing you can do is nothing.
Theodore Roosevelt

WHAT AND WHERE AND WHY

I keep six honest serving men
(They taught me all I know);
Their names are What and Why and When,
And How and Where and Who.
Rudyard Kipling

YOUR DESTINY AWAITS

Destiny is not a matter of chance; it is a matter of choice. It is not a thing to be waited for; it is a thing to be achieved.
William Jennings Bryan

SHAPING YOUR LIFE

Your philosophy is not best expressed in words; it is expressed in the choices you make. In the long run, you shape your life and you shape yourself. The process never ends until death. Your choices are ultimately your responsibility.
Eleanor Roosevelt

GETTING STARTED

Every accomplishment starts with the decision to try.
Author unknown

CHOOSE LIFE

Now choose life, so that you and your children may live and that you may love the Lord your God, listen to his voice, and hold fast to him.
Deuteronomy 30: 19–20 NIV

NO CHOICE?

When you have to make a choice, and don't make it, that is the choice.

William James

BECOMING YOURSELF

Every time you make a choice, you are turning the central part of you, the part that chooses, into something a little different from what it was before.

C. S. Lewis

CAN'T DECIDE?

We know what happens to people who stay in the middle of the road.

They get run over.

Author unknown

BE AN EXAMPLE FOR OTHERS

Don't let anyone think less of you because you are young, Be an example to all believers in what you teach, in the way you live, in your love, your faith, and your purity.

1 Timothy 4:12 NIV

YOU CAN ALWAYS MAKE A NEW CHOICE

Every moment you have a choice, regardless of what has happened before.

Choose right now to move forward, positively and confidently into your incredible future.

Author unknown

Prayer

Dear Lord, I feel brand new at making choices. Up to now, I've had a lot of guidance from family and friends and those who are invested in some way in my well-being and in my future. Now that I'm going out on my own, I ask You to stick close to me and help me make the decisions and the choices that will honor You. I've always been a person who wants to do the right thing, so guide me in my choices to continue to desire the good choice; or the right choice. Give me the wisdom to know when I've made a good choice, and if I make a poor choice, then help me get back on track quickly. Thank You for giving me the freedom to take a stand and to choose those things that move me toward my goals. Thank You for already preparing me to achieve my life purpose. Amen

Effort

The Energetic, Determined, and Effective You

*Let us therefore make every **effort** to do what leads to peace and mutual edification.*

Romans 14:19 NIV

Whew! You just got to the finish line, achieving a milestone goal, and now you're off and running again. Soon, you'll be trying new things. And to accomplish all that you want to do will require new energy and effort. You won't get to the triumph without a lot of "try" and a lot of "umph."

Making an effort and trying out new things means that sometimes you'll be pleased with the results and sometimes you won't. You may even be disappointed or annoyed that things didn't work out as you had hoped.

Perhaps the best way to pick yourself up and try again is to assume your prayer posture. Take the situation to God, explain what happened, and wait for some advice. Listen with your heart and mind. Try to see if you got ahead of what God wanted for you.

One of the great things about effort is that it comes with an eraser. You may imagine that you left erasers behind with school chalkboards, but the fact is God has a big eraser. He helps you fix the mistakes that you take to Him, so that you can renew your efforts later and try again.

Erasers are good because you can remove those parts that didn't work well and keep the parts that were effective. You don't have to start over, just work hard at getting things moving in the right direction.

You know when you put a lot of effort into something that is important to you. When your effort pays off, you move ahead; when it doesn't, you learn a life lesson. Either way, you haven't lost any time.

God loves every effort you make, so stay close to Him.

Keep going! You're doing great!

THE CHARACTER OF EFFORT

Hard work spotlights the character of people; some turn up their sleeves, some turn up their noses, and some don't turn up at all.

Author unknown

DO YOUR JOB WELL

If a person is called a street sweeper, he should sweep streets even as Michelangelo painted, or Beethoven composed music, or Shakespeare wrote poetry. He should sweep streets so well that all the hosts of heaven and earth will pause to say, "Here lived a great street sweeper who did his job well." *Martin Luther King Jr.*

FINDING HAPPINESS

Know that it is not the knowing, nor the talking, nor the reading person, but the doing person who at last will be found to be happy.

Author unknown

THE DIFFERENCE

After all is said and done, there's usually more said, than done!

Author unknown

A GREAT EFFORT

Work hard and cheerfully at whatever you do, as though you were working for the Lord rather than for people. *Colossians 3:23 NIV*

YOU ARE JUST ONE

I am only one, but still I am one.
I cannot do everything, but still I can do something;
and because I cannot do everything,
I will not refuse to do the something that I can do.

Edward Everett Hale

MAKE THE EFFORT

Take a method and try it. If it fails, admit it frankly, and try another. But by all means, try something.

Franklin Delano Roosevelt

ADD ENTHUSIASM

Nothing great was ever achieved without enthusiasm.

Ralph Waldo Emerson

GROWTH AND EFFORT

All growth depends upon activity. There is no development physically or intellectually without effort, and effort means work. Work is not a curse; it is the prerogative of intelligence, the only means to adulthood, and the measure of civilization.

Calvin Coolidge

Prayer

Dear Lord, I'm so excited about every possibility that is ahead of me, even about the things I hope and dream, but don't know exactly how to achieve. I thank You that You will be walking with me and helping me to work hard to accomplish my new goals. I pray that I will make every effort to please You as I forge a new path for my life. Keep me enthusiastic and give me the tools to do things well. There's so much to be done and I know that I cannot do any of it without You. You've helped me all along the way and I trust You to help me from here. Inspire my efforts in all my work.

Amen

Success

Success Comes in "Can"s

*Commit to the Lord whatever you do, and your plans will **succeed**.*

Proverbs 16:3 NIV

Graduation is certainly one kind of success. You got there by working hard, listening to others, and being willing to go the extra mile. You had a "can do" attitude.

One thing you may have discovered already is that dreams alone will not bring success. It's important to have a goal and to know what direction you want to go, but any achievement that comes your way will happen because of the things you do, the effort you are willing to expend.

Chances are that you will have numerous successes and failures as you take your life journey. Both of those are important ways to discover what you truly want. That's all good, but your greatest opportunity in life is to become the person God designed you to be.

If success could be purchased in beverage cans from a grocery store shelf, you might purchase a case of your favorite kinds, the ones that give you everything you want with just one sip. You could enjoy a refreshing moment with no effort at all. The blessing of God is that success does not come easily, and there is only one way to truly achieve it. Even if it doesn't come in grocery store cans, it still comes in "cans."

Success begins each time you say, "I can do this. I can seek God's help with my goals and dreams. I can try harder. I can find solutions. I can fix this. I can believe in myself. I can believe that God intends me to accomplish my work."

Every time you choose to say, "I can," you're on the right path. Of course, your success will not be as sweet unless you invite God into your plans and dreams right from the start. When you commit your work to the Lord, you know that He is with you guiding your plans and dreams.

There's no doubt that you are a "can do" person and that you will meet success face to face many times as you go through life. All you have to do is put your dreams into God's hands. He'll meet you right there. Now, get out there! You can do this!

LIVING YOUR LIFE

There is only one success—to be able to spend life in your own way.

Christopher Morley

TENTH FLOOR: SUCCESS!

For every person who climbs the ladder of success, there are a dozen waiting for the elevator.

Author unknown

DIVINE SUCCESS

It is not your business to succeed, but to do right; when you have done so, the rest lies with God.

C. S. Lewis

GREAT AND NOBLE ACHIEVEMENTS

I long to accomplish a great and noble task, but it is my chief duty to accomplish small tasks as if they were great and noble.

Helen Keller

DICTIONARY DEFINITION

The only place where success comes before work is in the dictionary.

Author unknown

KEEP LOOKING UP

As long as he sought the Lord, God gave him success.

2 Chronicles 26:5 NIV

TALK AND ACTION

You can't build a reputation on what you are going to do.

Henry Ford

MAY SUCCESS BEGIN

You become successful the moment you start moving toward a
worthwhile goal.   Author unknown

AIMING FOR SUCCESS

Aim at heaven and you will get earth thrown in.
Aim at earth and you will get neither.   C. S. Lewis

Prayer

*Father God, I have a few goals and some dreams. I don't know how any
of them will work out, but I ask Your guidance as I begin to find my way.
When I face obstacles that would cause me to doubt, strengthen and
renew my spirit. When I make an unwise choice, help me to discover it
quickly and get back on track.*

*I pray that You will watch over me and help me to succeed according
to Your will and purpose for my life. I seek Your grace and mercy and
whatever definition of success pleases You the most as You walk with me
through life. Thank You for bringing me this far. Help me to commit my
work to You and do the things that honor You as I go forward from here.*

Amen

Failure

Failure Only Means You Haven't Yet Succeeded

*Then I let it all out; I said, "I'll make a clean breast of my **failures** to God."*
Suddenly the pressure was gone—my guilt dissolved, my sin disappeared.

Psalm 32:5 MSG

Failure is personal. Only you can decide what qualifies as a disappointment or a failure in your life. Only you know the effort you made, or the story behind a door that closed, or the results that were less than you expected. The fact is that life itself will give you many opportunities to know what it feels like to succeed, and what it means to fail.

The stakes are a little different from the pass-fail system you may have had in school. Your grades were generally the result of the effort you put forth. As you get out into the world, though, you're in a competitive lineup with a lot of other people, and sometimes it will be for the same promotion or the same slot on a team or even for the same job. Not everyone can win in a competition.

Some would say that you should take "failure" out of your vocabulary; not even let it be an option. Maybe, but then you might miss the opportunity to grow or redefine yourself or understand what it means to truly succeed.

Those who play sports might tell you that you fail more than you win. Chances are good that you'll fail 100 percent of the times that you don't make an effort to take a shot.

When it comes to your faith, God wants you to take a shot at doing your best, turning your goals over to Him for care and keeping, and striving for something that is beyond your grasp. He wants you to think big—so big, in fact, that you are doomed to failure unless He intervenes. When you do that, it means you have put your faith in the front of the line. You have decided that trusting God for the things you want to achieve makes perfect sense. If God is for you, who can be against you?

Sometimes failure takes the form of rejection. Artists and writers and inventors and other creative people all know what it means to be rejected, to have failed. However, rejection is failure only if you stop there. If you continue to try, at some point you will achieve what you set out to do, or you will have defined a new goal and moved in a new direction.

Dealing with failure or disappointment or not achieving a goal has a silver lining. That ray of hope comes from your faith and the knowledge that God will continue to walk with you and lift you up until you get to the place you want to go. With God's help, you can turn those disappointments around and change them into stunning successes.

Keep going! You've got a lot of exciting things to do!

A GOOD THOUGHT

Sometimes a noble failure serves the world as faithfully as a distinguished success.
Author unknown

A QUESTION OF FAILURE

Did you stop trying because you failed, or did you fail because you stopped trying?
Author unknown

PONDER THIS

Our longest sorrows have an ending, and there is a bottom to the profoundest depths of our misery. Our winters shall not frown forever; summer shall soon smile. The tide shall not eternally ebb out; the floods must retrace their march. The night shall not hang in the darkness forever over our souls; the sun shall yet arise with healing beneath its wings.
C. H. Spurgeon

DON'T GIVE UP!

Never give in, never give in, never, never, never, never—in nothing, great or small, large or petty—never give in except to convictions of honor and good sense.
Winston Churchill

GOD'S GOOD PLANS

"For I know the plans I have for you," says the Lord, "They are plans for good and not for disaster, to give you a future and a hope."

Jeremiah 29: 11 NIV

HOPE PREVAILS

We must accept finite disappointment, but we must never lose infinite hope.

Martin Luther King Jr.

ATTITUDE ADJUSTMENT

Change is mandatory, stress is manageable, but misery is optional.

Author unknown

POINT OF VIEW

A pessimist sees the difficulty in every opportunity; an optimist sees the opportunity in every difficulty.

Winston Churchill

YOU CAN DO IT!

"Be strong and brave. Don't be afraid or discouraged."

1 Chronicles 22:13 NCV

Prayer

Dear Lord, it's humbling to stand before You, knowing that I've let You down. I missed the mark on the goals that we set together and now I need to find a new goal, make a new plan. I am sure there are things I could have done that may have influenced the outcome, but I'm not sure what that would have been. Though I am unhappy that I did not achieve my goal, I thank You that I can rest now and then begin again. Please help me face this difficult time with grace and help me to recognize what You would have me do from here.

I put my trust and my faith and my hope in You.

Amen

Goals

Just Do It!

*Stick with me, friends. Keep track of those you see running this same
course, headed for this same **goal**.* Philippians 3:17 MSG

The often-quoted Nike slogan is simple and direct. It's worth meditating
on whether you're looking at running a race, getting through school, or
working toward a job promotion. When it comes right down to it, there's
nobody who can "just do it" like you can. It's your personal goal.

Goals are never easily achieved. They seem to always come with obstacles, those things you have to climb over or around or through to get where
you want to go. The beauty of that obstacle course is that it defines your
goals even more because it causes you to be persistent. You're not willing
to let anything get in the way of your achievement. You're determined, and
those barriers only add to your desire to "Just do it!"

Brother Lawrence said, "All things are possible to the one who believes,
yet even more to the one who hopes, more still to the one who loves, and
most of all to the one who practices and perseveres in these three virtues."

As you move forward to your new goals, setting your plans and creating
your strategies to get there, remember that God wants to go with you. He
inspires your heart and mind toward the things you want to achieve, and
He can even help you get around and through some of those obstacles. He
wants you to continue to believe, and hope, and love.

You're on the way to making things happen, and with God's help, you
are sure to get there. Stay the course and keep going. Just do it!

OPENING DOORS

When one door closes, another door opens; but we often look so
long and so regretfully upon the closed door, that we do not see the
ones which open for us. Alexander Graham Bell

THE D.I.N. PRINCIPLE

Do It Now!   Dixie Oliver

WRITE DOWN YOUR GOALS

A written-down goal, in some way no one yet understands, tends to attract every ingredient it needs to realize it.   Author unknown

SEEK GOD'S BLESSING

Never undertake anything for which you would not have the courage to ask the blessing of heaven.   Georg Christoph Lichtenberg

GOD'S PURPOSE

For everything, absolutely everything, above and below, visible and invisible . . . everything got started in him and finds its purpose in him.   Colossians 1:16 MSG

BE THE BEST

Becoming a shining star in your chosen field may not be your destiny, but becoming the best person that you can be is a goal to always set for yourself.   Author unknown

YOU HAVE TO TRY

Only those who attempt the absurd achieve the impossible.
                                              Author unknown

GO FOR THE GOLD

So let us run the race that is before us and never give up.
                                              Hebrews 12:1 NCV

Prayer

Dear Lord, I don't know exactly what my goals should be, but I believe that You created me for a purpose, and so my first goal is to try to discover just what that purpose is. I pray that You will guide me toward

that end so that I can achieve the things that are in front of me in ways that please You. Help me to seek the advice of those who have gone before me, to be willing to think bigger than I've ever tried to think before, and to be willing to stay on the course that You set for me. I thank You for getting me this far and I trust that the possibilities and the opportunities before me will present themselves according to Your will and purpose. Thank You for going ahead of me and for helping me set my goals today.

Amen

Give

The Art of Giving

*God is the One who gives seeds to the farmer and bread for food. He will
give you all the seed you need and make it grow so there will be a great
harvest from your goodness.* 2 Corinthians 9:10 NCV

You already know a lot about what it means to be a giver. You have
learned that lending a helping hand to others benefits them, but it makes
you feel good too. You have given time to your friends simply because they
needed to share something with you, doing so even when you didn't have
a lot of time to spare. If you were to think of each opportunity to be giving
as a chance to plant seeds that will sprout and blossom in the future, then
you will see that your willingness to give comes back to you, and your happiness will grow with it.

Perhaps, too, you might consider the ways that God gives gifts to His
children—the way He gives gifts to you. He does it with an open hand
and an open heart. He does it even when He doesn't get a "thank you" in
return. He continues to give because God is love and He always treats His
children well. He gives unconditionally and generously.

Your spirit of generosity and giving is a reflection of the condition of your
heart. When you have a heart for God, you become more sensitive and
empathetic with His children. You bring words of encouragement and a
smile to those who feel disheartened. You give time and warm conversation to your friends. The art of giving is that your heart knows the joy of
making the day beautiful for those around you.

Winston Churchill said, "We make a living by what we get. We make a
life by what we give."

May your life be full of opportunities to share your heart and give your best to everyone you meet.

THE BLESSING

"You should remember the words of the Lord Jesus: 'It is more blessed to give than to receive.'"

Acts 20:35 NIV

WHAT CAN YOU GIVE?

Give strength, give thought,
Give deeds, give wealth;
Give love, give tears, and give yourself.
Give, give, be always giving.
Who gives not is not living;
The more you give, the more you live,
So give with all your heart.

Author unknown

THE FLINT, THE SPONGE, AND THE HONEYCOMB

Imagine three types of givers. One is a flint, one is a sponge, and one is a honeycomb. The flint giver must be hammered and chipped away before any spark of possible giving can occur. It has a fire inside but has become too hard-hearted to share its warmth.

The sponge giver must be squeezed into offering a drop of goodness and kindness to those around. The sponge giver quickly absorbs the gifts of others but doesn't offer a drop of possibility or hope or blessing when opportunities arise.

But the honeycomb giver simply overflows with sweetness and offers every drop of goodness to those around. The honeycomb giver reminds us of the way God gives. There is always more kindness and goodness and sweetness to share.

Adapted by K. Moore

A GOOD THOUGHT

Blessed are those who can give without remembering,
And those who can take without forgetting.

Author unknown

WHAT YOU HOLD

I have held many things in my hands, and I have lost them all.
Whatever I have placed in God's hands, I still possess.

Martin Luther

Prayer

*Dear Lord, You have been so generous to me. I pray that I will
remember all the ways You have added joy to my life. You have given me
good friends, and a good family. You've given me the chance to get an
education and the opportunity to grow and learn. You've put me in a
country where I am free to explore my own goals and dreams, and I'm
free to worship You as I choose. You've blessed me beyond measure and
given more to me than I can even recount. I pray that You will teach me
all that I can do to give back to my friends and family and to the work
of Your Kingdom. Thank You for being like the honeycomb, continually
nourishing me with the sweetness of Your Spirit.* Amen

Hope

When You Have Real Hope

*Faith means being sure of the things we **hope** for and knowing that something is real even if we do not see it.*
Hebrews 11:1 NCV

You have some experience with hope. When you were young, you may have hoped for some special event to happen on your birthday, or some special gift to be received at Christmas. You may have hoped to get on the basketball team as you grew up or hoped to get a perfect score on the SATs.

Now that you've graduated, you may have new hopes and dreams. You may recognize that your diploma means you can take advantage of other opportunities. It is a reality check in a way because it serves to show others that you've already accomplished something big in your life and so you can certainly have hope that you will accomplish more.

Faith and hope are often linked together as sharing in the vision we have for our lives. Faith assures us that we have every reason to hope for what we want because we don't have to see it to know it is possible. After all, as Saint Augustine wrote, "What can be hoped for which is not believed?"

As you move out into the world, remember what you believe and that you have every reason to hope in the One who designed your life. God is your anchor and He is your hope for all that you dream to be. He knows you better than you know yourself and so He can direct your steps and clear the path as you go forward. Your hope is built on His love and faithfulness. As it says in Romans 15:4 (NIV): "For everything that was written in the past was written to teach us, so that through the endurance taught in the Scriptures and the encouragement they provide we might have hope."

Wherever life takes you, be sure to draw near to God and continue in His Word. There you will find nuggets of hope when life lets you down. You will be blessed with renewed joy and hope as you follow Your Savior. Hold on to the vision He has given you. Let hope remain and chase away clouds of doubt when they appear, replacing them with streams of sunshine. When you choose to hope in God and His divine plan, all things are possible.

JOY AND PEACE

May the God of hope fill you with all joy and peace as you trust in him, so that you may overflow with hope by the power of the Holy Spirit.

Romans 15:13 NIV

HOPE IN THE BALANCE

The glory of the star, the glory of the sun—we must not lose either in the other. We must not be so full of the hope of heaven that we cannot do our work on the earth. We must not be so lost in the work of the earth, that we shall not be inspired by the hope of heaven.

Phillips Brooks

HOPE FOR US ALL

If seeds in the black earth can turn into such beautiful roses, what might not the heart of humankind become in its long journey toward the stars?

G. K. Chesterton

WINGS OF HOPE

Hope is the thing with feathers
That perches in the soul,
And sings the tunes without the words,
And never stops at all.

Emily Dickinson

HOPE AND HAPPINESS

Hope is itself a species of happiness, and perhaps the chief happiness which this world affords.

Samuel Johnson

DO IT WITH HOPE

Everything that is done in the world is done by hope. No gardener would sow a grain of corn if he hoped not it would grow up and become seed. No tradesman would set himself to work if he did not hope to reap the benefits of his labors.   Martin Luther

THROUGH SUN AND RAIN

Those who keep speaking about the sun while walking under a cloudy sky are messengers of hope, the true saints of our day.

Henri J.M. Nouwen

PRACTICE HOPE

Practice hope. As hopefulness becomes a habit, you can achieve a permanently happy spirit.   Norman Vincent Peale

Prayer

Dear Father in Heaven, You know I hope for a lot of things. I hope to do well in the world, discovering all that I am meant to do and be. I hope for the right work and the right opportunities. I hope for good friends and the support of my family.

You have given me many reasons to be hopeful already in the things I've done. Show me what you would have me do and lead me in hope toward the people and places where I belong. I put my hope in You, surrendering all my dreams and ideas into your hands and asking that You give back to me the ones that are truly mine. I thank You for giving me every reason for hope and joy.   Amen

Finding Success

That person is a success
Who has lived well, laughed often, and loved much;
Who has gained the respect of intelligent people and the love of children;
Who has filled a niche and accomplished a task;
Who leaves the world better than He found it.

adapted from Robert Louis Stevenson

Grow

Keep Going! Keep Growing!

When I was a child, I spoke and thought and reasoned as a child. But when I grew up, I put away childish things. 1 Corinthians 13:11 NLT

You are in growth mode. That means you're doing your best to learn quickly and well so that you can move forward in life. You grew through childhood, and you'll continue to learn how much you still need to know all through adulthood. It's just the way you were designed, because God never wants you to stop growing.

One writer said, "The head grows by taking in, but the heart grows by giving out." You've been busy the past few years "taking in," gaining head knowledge and learning more about yourself. You've discovered some of your strengths and some of your natural skills.

Your job here on planet Earth is to learn and to grow. You can have great book knowledge, but life will give you other ways to learn its mysteries. Only experience can teach you what you need to know. God wants your growth to be both physical and spiritual. He wants you to grow in your knowledge of Him. After you've gained considerable Bible knowledge, He wants you to transfer it all to your heart. He wants your heart to know Him, to grow big enough to contain Him.

Growing means you're willing to change, willing to try new things, take instruction from others, and be deliberate in your walk with God. Your growth will never be sufficient without Him because He designed you and He knows what you were made for. After all, as it says in Scripture, He is the Potter and you are the clay. What you become will be partly up to you and partly up to your spiritual growth. God has big plans for you and so

He wants you to walk with Him no matter what you're going through or what you choose to do with your life.

The challenge is on! Grow! Give God the glory!

DON'T STOP NOW

If you are pleased with what you are, you have stopped already. If you say, "It is enough," you are lost. Keep on walking, moving forward, trying for the goal. Don't try to stop on the way, or to go back, or to deviate from it.

Saint Augustine

LEAVING THE NEST

The mother eagle teaches her little ones to fly by making their nest so uncomfortable that they are forced to leave it and commit themselves to the unknown world of air outside. And just so does our God to us.

Hannah Whitall Smith

GROWING WITH GOD

As newborn babies want milk, you should want the pure and simple teaching. By it you can mature in your salvation, because you have already examined and seen how good the Lord is.

1 Peter 2:2–3 NCV

CHOOSE TO GROW

The strongest principle of growth lies in the human choice.

George Eliot

CONTINUE TO GROW

Mere change is not growth. Growth is the synthesis of change and continuity, and where there is no continuity, there is no growth.

C. S. Lewis

MAKING PROGRESS

I may not be who I want to be,
And I may not be who I am going to be,
But thank God, I am not who I was.

Author unknown

Prayer

Lord, I know I'm growing a little bit more each day. Sometimes I think growing up, being an adult, being in charge of my life, is a scary idea. Growing up seems to come with a lot of responsibility. I realize that is a good thing, but I know I need Your help to get there. I have grown in a lot of ways over the past couple years and I feel pretty good about where I am. I know that means I probably should get ready for a spurt of growth because I'm not going to stay in this spot very long. Watch over me, Lord, and help me to grow strong in my awareness of You before all other things. Amen

Peace

Give Peace a Chance

*And let the peace that comes from Christ rule in your hearts. For as members of one body you are called to live in **peace**.* Colossians 3:15 NLT

You may wonder if something like peace can actually exist in the world as you know it. Discord seems to rule the day, and the thought of waging peace, harmony, and just plain getting along seems to fall by the wayside. No matter how difficult it may appear to you, you can do something about peace, because it actually can start with you.

Peace is first waged in your heart, that is, you have to recognize that it's worth your time and effort. You can be an ambassador for peace by your kindness and your willingness to hear another point of view. You can give peace and harmony a chance in every social setting you are part of simply by not adding to the discord.

Of course, you need a few weapons to really wage peace: prayer, patience, and persistence. Prayer aligns your heart with God's purpose and keeps you mindful of what He wants you to do. Patience helps you allow others to speak their minds and hearts and then make your own decisions about what you might believe. Persistence is what it takes to wage anything for good. The funny thing about waging peace is that the first step is to put up the white flag and surrender—surrender to the God of the universe who rules and knows exactly the part He wants you to play.

Chaos may walk around your neighborhood, but you can keep peace in your home and in your heart. Give peace a chance!

LET NOTHING DISTURB YOU

Let nothing disturb you,
Nothing frighten you.

All things pass,
And God never changes.
When you endure things with patience,
You attain all things that God can give you.
When you have God,
You lack for nothing.   Teresa of Ávila

PEACE WITH GOD

Therefore, since we have been made right in God's sight by faith,
we have peace with God because of what Jesus Christ our Lord has
done for us.   Romans 5:1 NLT

PERSONAL PEACE

I couldn't live in peace if I put the shadow of a willful sin between
myself and God.   George Eliot

WHAT STEALS OUR PEACE?

We are not at peace with others because we are not at peace with
ourselves,

And we are not at peace with ourselves because we are not at
peace with God.   Thomas Merton

PEACE IS AN ACTION WORD

It isn't enough to talk about peace. One must believe in it.
And it isn't enough to believe in it. One must work at it.

Eleanor Roosevelt

FORGOTTEN PEACE

If we have no peace, it is because we have forgotten that we belong
to each other.   Mother Teresa

DISTRACTED?

We should have great peace if we did not busy ourselves with what
others say and do.   Thomas à Kempis

THE PEACEFUL PRESENT

A great many people are trying to make peace, but that has already been done. God has not left it for us to do; all we have to do is to enter into it.

Dwight L. Moody

Prayer

Lord God, I ask that you forgive anything within my heart that causes turmoil and anguish. I pray that You would replace any worries I have with Your peace. As you strengthen my life through Your peace, I pray that I would then share that peace with those around me, remembering that they, too, suffer from personal chaos when they are not connected to You. Bless each person who walks in peace, reminding others of who they are and how much they are loved by You, able even now to live in grace and harmony. Help me to be an ambassador of real peace in all that I do and say today.

Amen

Prayer

Please Hold, God Is Busy!

So I tell you to believe that you have received the things you ask for in prayer, and God will give them to you. Mark 11:24 NCV

Imagine that you called Heaven's Prayer Hotline and you were put on hold. "Oh, sorry! God is just swamped today, but He'll be back with you soon. You're currently number eighty-seven million six hundred and twenty-one. Your prayer requests are important to God, though, so please hold!"

At times, we're tempted to treat God like He has some heavenly switchboard operator who screens His calls and sends busy signals. We imagine that prayer comes with a lot of red tape or that God has much more important matters to deal with than our petty grievances. We hang up on God before He ever gets a chance to guide and direct us.

The fact is that there is no switchboard, and as soon as you call, you are number one! God hears you immediately, and because He anticipated your call, He's already at work to move your request along. Sure, sometimes you wait for His answer, but it's not because He's too busy; it's because you are! He knows that there are some things you have to do before He can answer your prayer so that it has His ultimate outcome. He gives you time to strengthen your position.

The more you and God communicate, the easier it is for Him to answer your prayers because you have a great relationship and He knows your heart. He loves to hear from you because you are His beloved child. You don't even have to call with a request. You can simply call to hear His voice and let Him know how much He means to you. In fact, you could do it right now. He's in and He's not too busy to take your call. He's waiting for you.

PRAYERS FROM THE HEART

Also, the Spirit helps us with our weakness. We do not know how to pray as we should. But the Spirit himself speaks to God for us, even begs God for us with deep feelings that words cannot explain. God can see what is in people's hearts. And he knows what is in the mind of the Spirit, because the Spirit speaks to God for his people in the way God wants.   Romans 8:26–27 NCV

PRAYER WARRIORS

A prayer warrior is a person who is convinced that God is omnipresent—that God has the power to do anything, to change anyone, and to intervene in any circumstance.

A person who truly believes this refuses to doubt God!

                                                              Author unknown

PRAYER ADVICE

If you're trying to get on your feet, get down on your knees.

                                                              Author unknown

A GOOD THOUGHT

If your prayers were always answered, you'd have reason to doubt the wisdom of God.   Author unknown

THE LORD'S PRAYER

Our Father in heaven,

    Hallowed be Your name.

    Your kingdom come. Your will be done on earth as it is in Heaven.

    Give us this day our daily bread, and forgive us our debts, as we forgive our debtors.

    And do not lead us into temptation, but deliver us from the evil one.

    For Yours is the kingdom and the power and the glory forever. Amen.   Matthew 6:9–13 NKJV

THE PRACTICE OF PRAYER

What can be more excellent than prayer? What is more profitable to our life? What is sweeter to our souls, more sublime, in the course of our whole life, than the practice of prayer? Saint Augustine

MORNING AND EVENING PRAYERS

In the morning, prayer is the key that opens to us the treasures of God's mercies and blessings; in the evening, it is the key that shuts us up under His protection and safeguard. Henry Ward Beecher

ASK, SEARCH, KNOCK

Ask, and you will receive, Search, and you will find. Knock, and the door will be opened for you. Everyone who asks will receive. Everyone who searches will find. And the door will be opened for everyone who knocks. Matthew 7:7–8 CEV

GIVE GOD A CALL

All who call on God in true faith, earnestly from the heart, will certainly be heard, and will receive what they have asked and desired, although not in the hour or in the measure, or the very thing which they ask; yet they will obtain something greater and more glorious than they had dared to ask. Martin Luther

Prayer

Father in Heaven, I am still a novice when it comes to prayer. I may have graduated from school, but I still need to be educated about the ways I can come to Your throne. I ask You to teach me how to pray in ways that please You and in ways that serve others. I offer my heart to You as You listen to my words, praying that You would hear each message through the gift of the Holy Spirit. Help me to be a persistent and consistent person of prayer so that I build my relationship with You and so we can get to know each other better. Amen

Love

Lessons in Love

Love is more important than anything else. It is what ties everything completely together.
Colossians 3:14 CEV

If Love 101 were a college course, you'd sign up and get an overview of some of the best definitions from poets and writers and philosophers galore. You'd probably talk about love as a description of someone's passion for the theater or baseball because, in their fervor, they never miss a show, or they talk about their team in nearly every conversation.

You'd talk about familial love, the kind you have for your heritage and your close family members. It's a bond that is different than any other love you might experience. Of course, you'd cover romantic love and all the ups and downs that it brings, probably leaving that part of the course no wiser than when you began.

There are a lot of lessons about love. And since God is love by definition, then it suits us to learn more about what that means. If God is love, then what does He expect us to know about love? Jesus told His followers that the key to love was to love God with your heart, soul, and mind, and to love others as you love yourself. That should cover every person on the planet and the ones in Heaven, so love is a big deal.

We know for sure that "love" is an action verb. It requires you to do something about it. If you love God, then you are expected to show Him that you do, and you've been given many ways to do that. You can read His Word to learn more about Him, you can pray so that you build your relationship, and you can live in a way that pleases Him, telling others about Him as you go.

As you grow to know more about love, keep in mind that the world is full of imitations. There are many who aspire toward love but are far from grasping the kind of compassion, energy, respect, and genuine effort that love requires. As you go through Love 101, take some notes because you are going to be amazed at how much there is to learn.

One thing is for sure: You are loved! God will never let anything come between His love for you and the life you live in the world. His love is steadfast and unconditional. Bring up those words in Love 101, and see what kind of discussion follows. Love is the key to everything!

WHY GOD LOVES YOU

God loves you not because of who you are, but because of who He is!

Author unknown

GOD SO LOVED YOU

For God so loved the world that he gave his one and only Son, that whoever believes in him shall not perish but have eternal life.

John 3:16 NIV

THE GOAL OF LOVE

Love is the fulfillment of all our works. There is the goal; that is why we run. We run towards it and once we reach it, in it we shall find rest.

Saint Augustine

LOVE IS A HUG

Love is always open arms. With arms open you allow love to come and go as it will, freely, for it'll do so anyway. If you close your arms about love, you'll find you are left holding only yourself.

Leo Buscaglia

LOVE BUILDS CHARACTER

Love is not a thing of enthusiastic emotion. It is a rich, strong, vigorous expression of the whole round Christian character—the Christ-like nature in its fullest development. And the constituents of this great character are only to be built up by ceaseless practice.

Henry Drummond

BEING LOVED

The greatest happiness of life is the conviction that we are loved—
Loved for ourselves, or rather, loved in spite of ourselves.

Victor Hugo

LOVE'S MIRACLE

This is the miracle that happens every time to those who really
love: The more they give, the more they possess.

Rainer Maria Rilke

Prayer

*Father in Heaven, I know that I have a lot to learn about love. I ask that
you guide me in the ways of love so that I will be a compassionate and
kind person to those around me. I pray that you will give me wisdom in
romantic love so that I will know how to protect it and appreciate it for
the gift that it truly is.*

*I pray, Lord, that I will learn to love You in greater measure, putting
You first in my life and seeking to share my heart with Yours. I also ask
that You help me to love myself, not because I am special, but because
You created me in Your image, and so I need to love myself more that I
might love you more too. Thank You, Lord, for your many gifts of love.*

Amen

Guide

God Goes Ahead of You

*By day the LORD went ahead of them in a pillar of cloud to **guide** them on their way and by night in a pillar of fire to give them light, so that they could travel by day or night.*   Exodus 13:21 NIV

You're probably familiar with getting guidance, direction, instruction on what to do next because that's part of the job of educational systems. Teachers and guidance counselors and coaches are all there to keep moving you forward, guiding you toward that big day of graduation. It is time and effort well spent.

Now, though, as you go out into the world, there will not be as many people looking out just for you. It won't be anyone's job to simply be sure you get to the next step and that you're advised as to the best ways to get there. Sure, your parents will perhaps share their thoughts about your life direction, but you will have to decide what to do from here.

The good news is that you are not going on alone. Now you will look for guidance from your Heavenly Father, the One who knows you better than you know yourself. You will look to Him by day and again by night and He will give you insights and wisdom. He will offer you discernment and opportunities to make choices that can make a difference.

When you aren't quite sure where to get guidance, or whom you should really listen to, then go back to what you already know: that God waits to teach you and show you the way. Sit down and ask yourself what Jesus would do in your situation. Once you've figured that out, then seek more counsel because the best success comes from getting good advice.

Just as God went before the people of Israel as they walked through the desert, He goes before you, making sure that you will arrive safely at each destination. Give God the thanks for guiding you along the path of life.

GOOD TO KNOW

I am satisfied that when the Almighty wants me to do or not to do any particular thing, He finds a way of letting me know.

Abraham Lincoln

WHICH WAY?

The strength and happiness of a person consists in finding out the way in which God is going and going that way too.

Henry Ward Beecher

A GOOD QUESTION

Happy the soul which by a sincere self-renunciation, holds itself ceaselessly in the hands of its Creator, ready to do everything which He wishes; which never stops saying to itself a hundred times a day, "Lord, what would you have me do?"

François Fenélon

KEEPING IN STEP

Since we live by the Spirit, let us keep in step with the Spirit.

Galatians 5:25 NIV

TRAINING GROUND

Direct your children onto the right path, and when they are older, they will not leave it.

Proverbs 22:6 NLT

UNDERSTANDING WILLPOWER

You give God your will, and He gives you His power.

Author unknown

GUIDANCE FROM OTHERS

The next best thing to being wise yourself is to live in a circle of those who are.

C. S. Lewis

WHEN GOD GUIDES

When God is your guide,
He will always provide

Each thing that you need
To do a great deed,
Because He is there by your side.   K. Moore

Prayer

Dear Lord, if I was going on a trip, I'd probably try to buy a good guide book so that I could discover ahead of time where to go and what to do. On this trip of life, I ask that I might understand more of what You would have me do with the help of my Holy Bible, Your guidebook. I know that with You beside me, I can go anywhere on earth and you'll be there ready to assist my goals and my steps. Walk with me, Lord, as I go my way each day, and be my friend and my guide, for I know that I would be lost without You.   *Amen*

Work

Who's the Boss?

Work willingly at whatever you do, as though you were working for the Lord rather than for people.   Colossians 3:23 NLT

One of the key reasons you invest time in education is so that you can get a better job. Without a diploma, certain jobs are not even available to you. Without a higher degree, you may not even get an interview, no matter how skilled you may be. Most of your life is spent in training for the job you will do. Even after you land the job, the training continues. Now and then, you may lose your job, get downsized, or simply decide it wasn't the right fit for you. You may lose a job, but you will never be out of work.

When you choose to work for the Lord, you always have an opportunity to be in business. Your work is to tell His stories and share your heart about the amazing things He has done in your life. Your work is so far-reaching that it will always be available to you no matter how old you are because there's no need to retire. God can use you anytime you're willing to volunteer for the job He has in mind.

If you're wondering whether you'll get paid for your work, you might consider this. You have already received a sizable inheritance just by becoming a child of God. Beyond that, you have an awesome Boss who can do more for you than any earthly boss could ever do. You'll have health benefits and spiritual benefits and a kind of peace that few possess in any job they might have.

Your services are always welcome, always appreciated, but never required. God wants your heart even more than He wants your help. He's working on the best plan for your life that is possible. No matter what job you may have in the world, keep your heart in your work and God will bless what you do.

DEPOSIT SLIPS

You can draw nothing out of the bank of life, unless you put
something into it.   Author unknown

GO FOR IT!

Whatever you can do or dream you can, begin it.
Boldness has genius, power, and magic in it.

Johann Wolfgang von Goethe

IT'S ALL GOOD!

All labor that uplifts humanity has dignity and importance and
should be undertaken with painstaking excellence.

Martin Luther King Jr.

DO YOUR WORK WELL

Whatever work you do, do your best.   Ecclesiastes 9:10 NCV

IT'S A PIECE OF CAKE!

Do you think the work God gives you to do is never easy? Jesus
says His yoke is easy. His burden is light. People sometimes refuse
to do God's work just because it is easy. This is sometimes because
they cannot believe that easy work is His work.   George MacDonald

WORTHY WORK

Far and away the best prize that life offers is the chance to work
hard at work worth doing.   Theodore Roosevelt

A THOUGHT TO PONDER

We have worked, we have even worked hard;
But the question comes to us; "What have we worked for?
Who has been our master? With what object have we toiled?"

C. H. Spurgeon

Prayer

Lord, I'm just beginning to really consider the kind of job I hope to have in the world. I have a lot of questions and very few answers. I pray that You will direct my steps as I discover more of the work I am meant to do. I pray that You will bless the work of my hands. Thank You that I can join Your team of believers and go forward knowing that You are with me. Help me to know when to share stories about You with others and grant that I might recognize the opportunities to work for You all the days of my life. I'm grateful for every blessing You have shared with me.

Amen

Knowledge

What Do You Really Know?

*The mind of a person with understanding gets **knowledge**; the wise person listens to learn more.*　　　　　　　　　　　Proverbs 18:15 NCV

Here you are, a fresh diploma in your hand and ready to face the world. According to that degree you just earned, you know things. You know lots of things. Okay, so now what?

Perhaps part of what is ahead of you is to discover what kind of knowledge you really have. Do you have a lot of great information in your head that will allow you to recite poetry or facts of history or create an awesome scientific formula? Do you have a talent for art or dance and so you know something about those two areas that few others might know?

Whatever knowledge you may have right now, it's safe to say that there's plenty more where that came from. You've got years of reading and thinking and growing to do, and all of it will serve you well. God has blessed you with a good mind and heart, and He fully respects your efforts and expects you to keep growing, in every way.

The other form of knowledge that will still take a lot of hard work is in shaping your awareness and your true understanding as you get to know God. Knowing God doesn't come with a PhD program, but it does come with perks and lifetime guarantees, actually eternal guarantees.

You're at the beginning of the greatest adventure of your life. You're out to gain knowledge of the world and discover how the world can serve you as you serve God. You need head knowledge in your chosen field, and you need heart knowledge so that you can create lasting relationships. You

also need to know God, because only He can help you with every other thing you hope to accomplish.

He has a lot for you to discover and He's an awesome teacher. May you be blessed with every step you take to truly get to know the One who will forever be your guide.

Getting knowledge is good; getting to know God is better!

PERSPECTIVE

Knowledge is proud to know so much;
Wisdom is humbled to know so little. Author unknown

WHAT WE DON'T KNOW

We don't know a millionth of one percent about anything.

Thomas Edison

KNOWLEDGE IS A MYSTERY

As we acquire more knowledge, things do not become more comprehensible, but more mysterious. Albert Schweitzer

SOLOMON'S PRAYER

Now give me wisdom and knowledge so I can lead these people in the right way, because no one can rule them without your help.

2 Chronicles 1:10 NCV

ANCIENT WISDOM

True knowledge exists in knowing that you know nothing;
And in knowing that you know nothing, that makes you the smartest of all. Socrates

CURIOSITY

People can go anywhere, do everything and be completely curious about the universe.

Only a rare person now and then is curious enough to want to know God. A. W. Tozer

GROWING IN KNOWLEDGE

When I was young, I was sure of everything;

In a few years, having been mistaken a thousand times, I was not half so sure of most things as I was before;

At present, I am hardly sure of anything but what God Has revealed to me.

John Wesley

ONE MORE THOUGHT

Beware that you are not swallowed up in books!

An ounce of love is worth a pound of knowledge.

John Wesley

Prayer

Dear Lord, as I stand here now and talk with You, I realize that I've got a long way to go to be even reasonably intelligent. My knowledge is certainly limited and the little bits of information I possess are just drops in the ocean of all that You would have me know. I ask that You help me to use what I've learned so far, wisely and well.

Give me the right perspective and the desire to learn more when I'm in over my head. Help me to recognize those times when I need to do more research and gather more information before I jump into anything. Keep me from trusting myself without first bringing my plans and ideas to You. I look forward to learning all that You have to teach me so that I can know You and Your purpose for my life.

Amen

Action

What Will You Do from Here?

*Dear children, let's not merely say that we love each other; let us show the
truth by our **actions**. Our actions will show that we belong to the truth, so
we will be confident when we stand before God.*   1 John 3:18–19 NLT

As your graduation celebration becomes a warm memory, you'll start
looking ahead to determine what's next. Every time you complete one
project or goal, it's time to create a new one, time to take new action steps.
You may have some of those first steps figured out. You'll get an advanced
degree, or you'll get a job, or you'll travel a bit and then begin a new course
for your life.

Before you do anything, take a moment and just breathe. You've worked
hard to accomplish your graduation goals, and now you're prepared to
discover more about yourself and what your life purpose might be. That's
all good, but maybe the most important thing you can do is simply stop
everything. Breathe in and breathe out and remind yourself that you're
exactly where you should be.

Sit quietly with God. That action alone could make a big difference
in where you'll go from here and what you'll do next. Prepare to dream a
little bigger, listen a little longer, and even confess any anxieties you may
have about creating the best possible life.

Think about all that you've learned and then look at what you already
know. You have a better sense of what you're good at and at those things
that just will never interest you. You have a glimpse of things that you
might like to pursue sometime later. Every gift you've been given will find
its opportunity as you choose to act upon it.

Sometimes we run too quickly, and things don't work out as we
intended. By choosing to simply stay still and listen to God, that one

action may change each step you take after today. You've got a lot to think about but remember that you will never have to go anywhere alone. God loves you and will be at your side whatever you choose to do from here.

TO DO OR NOT TO DO

"I must do something" will always solve more problems than "Something must be done."

Author unknown

TAKE ACTION

Procrastination and worry are twin thieves that will try to rob you of your brilliance—
But even the smallest action will drive them away from you.

Author unknown

MAKING A DIFFERENCE

Act as if what you do makes a difference.
It does!

William James

A WIN OR LOSE ATTITUDE

The probability that we may fail in the struggle ought not to deter us from the support of a cause we believe to be just.

Abraham Lincoln

OPPORTUNITIES ABOUND

One drop of water helps to swell the ocean,
A spark of fire helps to give light to the world.
None are too small, too feeble, too poor to be of service.
Think of this and act!

Hannah More

TOO MUCH TO DO?

The shortest way to do many things is to do one thing at once!

Samuel Smiles

ACTION AND FAITH

We are not made righteous by doing righteous deeds;
But when we have been made righteous, we do righteous deeds.

Martin Luther

DOING GOOD DEEDS

If anyone, then, knows the good they ought to do and doesn't do it,
it is sin for them.

James 4:17 NIV

Prayer

Dear Lord, I'm excited about the plans I've made. I can't wait to try some new things and do what I believe I'm meant to do. I know that things could change, or You may have another direction for me, but I'm happy to get started and see where it goes. Help me to act in ways that honor You and my family. Remind me to think through the steps I want to take before I do anything. I know that I sometimes act impulsively. I pray that You will always be close to me and that You will let me know pretty clearly when I've moved away from You or I've gone down a trail that You don't think is wise. When that happens, help me to listen to You and not be stubborn. I know that You want to work all things out for my good, and so I trust You for all I do from here. Amen

Wisdom

Whatever Happened to Common Sense?

*But if any of you needs **wisdom**, you should ask God for it. He is generous to everyone and will give you wisdom without criticizing you.*

James 1:5 NCV

No doubt you've already been around people who simply don't exhibit sound judgment. They take chances that could be devastating. They live with reckless abandon as though life has no consequences at all. To put it simply, they don't have an ounce of what we might call common sense.

Few people actually talk about having wisdom today. We might consider our life direction with sober thought or we might try to understand the ways of others so that we can develop greater insight into ourselves, but few of us strive to attain wisdom.

Remember the day that Solomon became king after his father, David? God anointed Solomon and gave him the opportunity to ask God for anything that he might want. God did this because He loved his servant David and wanted to honor David's son.

After considering God's question, Solomon asked for just one thing... wisdom. He knew that he could not rule Israel without being able to understand the people, perceiving their hearts so that he would know what to do in every situation.

It turns out, God was impressed. He was pleased that Solomon did not ask for a long life, or greater riches, or to be successful in every battle. Instead, he asked to be wise. God gave him greater wisdom than any human being has had before or since. He gave him everything else as well, from riches to long life.

God wants you to be discerning, perceptive, insightful, and wise. He wants you to know when you need Him and when you need to take steps to fulfill His purpose. He wants you to be more than smart, more than knowledgeable; He wants you to be wise.

May God bless you with great wisdom for every step you take from here.

COMMON SENSE

Common sense is genius dressed in working clothes.

Author unknown

THE HEART OF WISDOM

Those who have the largest hearts have the soundest understandings,
> And the truest philosopher is the person who can forget himself.

William Hazlitt

USE YOUR TIME WISELY

Teach us to use wisely all the time we have.   Psalm 90:12 CEV

UNDERSTANDING

It is the province of knowledge to speak.
And it is the privilege of wisdom to listen.

Oliver Wendell Holmes Sr.

THE WISE OLD OWL

A wise old owl sat on an oak,
The more he saw, the less he spoke.
The less he spoke, the more he heard,
Why aren't we like that wise old bird?   Edward Hersey Richards

WISDOM AND FOOLISHNESS

Do not fool yourselves. If you think you are wise in this world, you should become a fool so that you can become truly wise, because the wisdom of this world is foolishness with God.

It is written in the Scriptures, "He catches those who are wise in their own clever traps."

It is also written in the Scriptures, "The Lord knows what wise people think. He knows their thoughts are just a puff of wind."

1 Corinthians 3:18–20 NCV

PROVERBIAL WISDOM

Wise sayings are like great teachers talking to us. They are the cheapest consultants, advisers, guidelines, pilots, signposts, guardians, and counselors we can find.

They make us wise more quickly than any other source of knowledge.

In short, they are direct lines to wisdom.   Adapted by K. Moore

Prayer

Dear Lord, I admit I probably wouldn't have been wise enough to ask You for wisdom like Solomon did. I might have thought it would be better to have a bigger army or a greater treasure. Even though I won't be ruling over any other people, help me to be smart enough to come to You for guidance and wisdom in the things I do.

From what I've learned so far, I can see that it's pretty easy to be foolish. Foolishness seems to follow people around and strike at any moment. It slips into the ego and then it makes a person do things that only brings them sorrow a little later on. I confess that I'm bound to take the foolish path now and then.

As I go forward from this day, though, I pray that I will be wise enough to know when I'm wrong, when I need to say, "I'm sorry," and when I need to come to You for guidance. I ask these things in Jesus' name.

Amen

Truth

In the Name of Truth

*But when the Spirit of **truth** comes, he will lead you into all truth. He will not speak his own words, but he will speak only what he hears, and he will tell you what is to come.*   John 16:13 NCV

It has been said: "If you don't learn to know your truths, you cannot speak them. If you don't speak them, you may lock them up inside yourself. If you tell the truth to yourself and then share it with others, the truth will set you free."

This observation may ring true for many people, but Jesus took this thought even further. He said, "You will know the truth and the truth will set you free." Jesus wasn't talking about whatever you imagine or deem to be your own truth. He was talking about knowing God, the truth of God, the fact of God, and that once you understand clearly that God is everything He has promised to be, then God's truth will free you of any lies you may have told yourself.

The truth will set you free. That's an amazing thought and one that you will want to sit with and meditate upon in your quiet time. Sometimes in your life, you'll be relieved that the truth is a foundation stone that supports all that you are and all that you hope to be. The truth brings out the best, the most important, and the factual aspects of life, and puts them before you.

When you're faced with truth, God comes ever nearer so that He can guide you as you respond to what you've learned. When you come to know that God is real, that He stands on His promises, and that His love for you is the greatest truth you will ever know, then your heart and mind will be free. The weight of the world will disappear because you will rest in the gift of God's grace, mercy, and truth.

As you leave your formal education behind, give yourself permission not only to grow in knowledge and wisdom as you meet the world, but to also declare those things that are without any doubt God's truth for your life. May you be blessed beyond measure.

TRUTH AND LOVE

Truth is the greatest gift of life, and love is the sweetest exercise of that truth.

Author unknown

GOD'S HONEST TRUTH

When I found truth, there I found my God, Who is truth itself.
And since I discovered God, He has lived in my mind and heart.
When any doubts assail me, I simply find truth again resting peacefully in my soul.

Adapted from Saint Augustine

TRUTH STANDS ALONE

The truth is incontrovertible.
Malice may attack it.
Ignorance may decide it.
But in the end, there it is.
It stands alone!

Adapted from Winston Churchill

TRUTH'S OPPOSITION

If a million people believe a foolish thing, it is still a foolish thing.

Anatole France

TRUTH IN WISDOM

Truth is the first chapter in the book of wisdom.

Thomas Jefferson

TRUTH BE TOLD

We believe that the truth is more than a system;
But we also believe that the truth is one, even as God is one.
And we believe, therefore, that the truth is systematic,
And that the different truths are all related.

C. S. Lewis

DEFENDING TRUTH

Not to oppose error is to approve of it. Not to defend truth is to suppress it.

Pope Felix III

Prayer

Father in Heaven, You know that the world is full of distractions and philosophies and opinions that are broadcast on social media and intended to appear as truth. Most of those things are fake news, false advertising, and far away from anything that might resemble truth. Yet we put them in our heads and wonder what to do with them.

I pray today that You would keep me grounded in Your truth no matter what news feed comes across my computer screen or what ideas come from the voices of friends. Help me to know You and Your truth in such a way that nothing can put a wedge between us. Keep me safely in Your care as I learn to differentiate Your voice from the voices of the world.

Amen

The Prayer of
Saint Francis of Assisi

Lord, make me an instrument of your peace.
Where there is hatred, let me sow love.
Where there is injury, pardon.
Where there is doubt, faith.
Where there is despair, hope.
Where there is darkness, light.
Where there is sadness, joy.
Grant that I may not seek so much to be consoled, as to console;
Not so much to be understood, as to understand;
Not so much to be loved, as to love.
For it is in giving that we receive,
It is in pardoning, that we are pardoned;
It is in dying that we are born to eternal life.

Teaching

Your Education Goes On

*The **teachings** of the LORD are perfect; they give new strength. The rules of the LORD can be trusted; they make plain people wise.* Psalm 19:7 NCV

You've had many teachers over the years; some memorable because they were less than you might have hoped they would be, and some memorable because they knew how to reach into your heart and mind and cause you to think and develop informed opinions. They prepared you for the future.

Teaching comes with great responsibility, and good teachers provide a rich environment for learning more than content. They want you to come away from their classes with understanding, perspective, and even the desire to know more.

As you go into the world, you'll find teachers everywhere. Some will offer you amazing insight and opportunity to discover new ideas. Some will be teaching views that are contrary to your faith. You will have to be good at discerning the difference between those who would hinder your faith and those who pose ideas that will encourage your walk with God. Perhaps one way to note the difference is identified in the above Scripture. It says that the teachings of the Lord are perfect, and because they are perfectly right for you, they will give you new strength.

Wherever you go from here, seek the teaching of the Lord. Look for a Bible study in your neighborhood or at your school or place of business. Find a church where you can be involved with learning more of the Word that can be trusted to give you wisdom and guidance and opportunities to know God better.

It may be tempting to put aside this kind of teaching as you go on with your new life, but if you persist in learning who you are as a child of God, you will discover that it is relevant to every area of your life from here to Heaven.

May you be blessed by good teaching even as you leave formal education behind.

ONE LESSON AT A TIME

For precept must be upon precept,
Precept upon precept; line upon line,
Line upon line; here a little, and there a little.

Isaiah 28:10 JKV

FISHING LESSON

Give a person a fish and he will eat for day,
Teach a person to fish and he will eat for a lifetime.

Author unknown

INFLUENCE ABOUNDS

A teacher affects eternity; there's no way to tell where the teacher's influence stops.

Henry B. Adams

GRATITUDE FOR TEACHING

Our critical day is not the very day of our death,
But the whole course of our life;
I thank them, that pray for me when my bell tolls;
But I thank them much more, that catechize me,
Or preach to me or instruct me how to live.

John Donne

TEACHER'S REPORT CARD

The mediocre teacher tells.
The good teacher explains.
The superior teacher demonstrates.
The great teacher inspires.

William A. Ward

YOUR MEMORY VERSE

"My God, I want to do what you want. Your teachings are in my heart."

Psalm 40:8 NCV

Prayer

Lord, You've been teaching me my whole life. You instructed me through the voices of my parents. You helped me discover more about myself through my friends and through my formal education. You corrected me when I started to go in the wrong direction. You've been with me every step of the way, and I have grown stronger, encouraged by Your Word and blessed by all that I've learned.

I know that others will be teaching me new ideas and offering me new points of view as I leave the protection of family and formal education behind. I ask that You guard me as I go, helping me to stand fast and hold on to what I already know about You, shining a light on my future so that I can one day teach others about You as well.   Amen

Forgive

Graduate from Grudges

*Then Peter came to him and asked, "Lord, how often should I **forgive** someone who sins against me? Seven times?"*

"No, not seven times," Jesus replied, "but seventy times seven!"

Matthew 18:21–22 NLT

You may wonder why "forgive" is one of the great words you need now that you're a graduate. After all, you want to be inspired and motivated and offered insight into what is ahead. Martin Luther King Jr. said, "Forgiveness is not an occasional act; it is an attitude."

Chances are good then as you go forward that your forgiveness attitude will be tested. Perhaps you still have some baggage from your school years. Maybe you still harbor some resentment for the kid who got the part you wanted in the school play, or the one who somehow always edged you out on test scores. You may still suffer over the person you wanted to date, or that you weren't picked for a royal moment at the prom.

Now that you're starting over, leaving all this behind, it's a good opportunity to ask God to help you forgive those who offended you, and to help you remember those moments when you needed to seek someone else's forgiveness.

You can't change the past, but you can change the future. Letting go of the stories from yesterday will give you a clean slate and remove the weight of disappointment and disillusion from your mind and heart.

God knows how weak you are, and He knows you make a lot of mistakes. An attitude that remembers how many times you have been forgiven already by the Creator of the universe may just help you be a person who is willing to pardon, make amends, and forgive someone else too.

The future looks a lot lighter now, and while you're adopting a more forgiving attitude, don't forget to forgive yourself. Time for a new start! You've got a clean slate. Move on!

LIGHTER AND BRIGHTER

Two things that will set you free and make your heart light: Forgive and you too will be forgiven; and give and you will receive. It's a formula for success.   Adapted from Saint Augustine

MARTIN LUTHER'S DREAM

In a dream Martin Luther once had he saw a book where all his sins were written. In the dream, the devil spoke to Luther, "Martin, here is one of your sins, here is another," pointing to the writing in the book. Then Luther said to the devil, "Take a pen and write, 'The blood of Jesus Christ, God's Son, cleanses us from all sin.'"

NO FISHING

God has cast our confessed sins into the depths of the sea, and He's even put a "No Fishing" sign over the spot.   Dwight L. Moody

VACANCY IN HEAVEN

If God were not willing to forgive sin, Heaven would be empty.
                                            Author unknown

CLOTHED IN OUR RIGHT MINDS

Dear Lord and Father of mankind,
Forgive our foolish ways,
Reclothe us in our rightful mind,
In purer lives your service find,
In deeper reverence, praise!   John Greenleaf Whittier

GOD KNOWS YOU

The Lord is like a father to his children, tender and compassionate to those who fear him.

For he knows how weak we are; he remembers we are only dust.
                                            Psalm 103:13–14 NLT

THE FRAGRANCE OF FORGIVENESS

Forgiveness is the fragrance the violet sheds on the heel that has crushed it.

Mark Twain

Prayer

Lord, You know that I still have a few stories in my head that focus on my disappointment with a friend, or my sense of injustice over some petty thing that happened. I don't want to take those grudges, those negative thoughts, with me as I leave my school days behind.

I pray that anyone I may have offended during these years will find it in their hearts to forgive me now. I pray that I will truly forgive and forget forever any of the slights or hurtful moments I might still be carrying around with me. I know, Lord, that You have forgiven me many things and I also know that I don't do anything to earn Your forgiveness, so let me keep that in mind all the rest of my life as issues of forgiveness come about. Thank You for helping me to build a forgiving attitude.

Amen

Learning

Get into the Game

*Let the wise listen and add to their **learning**, and let the discerning get guidance.*

Proverbs 1:5 NIV

During your academic years, you got a sense of how well you learned a particular topic when you were tested and ranked among your classmates. Sometimes you were graded on a bell curve, which may have given you an advantage when you weren't doing as well with the subject matter. Other times you did well on an exam, but you didn't know the subject beyond what you learned for the test. You were good at figuring out the questions, so you could provide the right answers.

Now that you've graduated, there won't be a simple scoring system or a weekly test to help you define how well you know important material. Now you'll have to test yourself and assess your own abilities. You've learned a lot, and though you may not intend to further your formal education, your learning will never cease. You'll quickly discover that being a brilliant math student may not help you become brilliant at life skills.

For that, you need to get in the game—the game of life, that is.

Henry Ford said, "Anyone who stops learning is old, whether at twenty or at eighty."

You have to embrace learning and get in the game. You won't gain many skills from the sidelines, so it's best to get right into the middle of it. The good news is that you have an incredibly talented Coach. In fact, He knows every play and every move you should make. He's given you a Playbook for your ready reference, and anytime you choose to consult with Him on how the game is going, He will be right there with you. Sometimes He'll give you a new game plan; other times He'll protect and guard you by taking you in an unexpected direction. No matter what, if you let Him call the plays, you will find yourself at the finish line, victorious. It's a game you are sure to win.

Wherever you plan to go from here, get in the game, keep up with your Coach, and practice, practice, practice! You will learn more than you ever dreamed possible, and you'll never need to be graded on a bell curve. You're already one of His star students.

GET IN THE GAME

Learning is not a spectator sport.   Author unknown

DIFFICULT LESSONS

Personally, I'm always ready to learn, although I do not always like being taught.   Winston Churchill

FOUNTAIN OF YOUTH

Anyone who keeps learning stays young.
The greatest thing in life is to keep your mind young.   Henry Ford

LABELED LEARNERS

A boy was expelled from his Latin class because he was a slow learner. He resolved to excel in English where he was slow in Latin. His name was Winston Churchill.

A six-year-old boy was sent home from school with a note saying he was too stupid to learn. His name was Thomas Edison.

Sir Walter Scott's teacher called him a hopeless dunce.

Louis Pasteur was considered to be the slowest learner in his chemistry class.

Keep learning!

LOVE LEARNING

Those who get wisdom do themselves a favor, and those who love learning will succeed.   Proverbs 19:8 NCV

AN ATTITUDE FOR LEARNING

True education doesn't merely bring us learning,
But love of learning; not merely preparation for work, but love of
work.   Author unknown

Prayer

*Dear Master Teacher, I am humbled by what You've shown me so far
about how to learn new things and how to apply what I learn to life
itself. I'm a long way from truly understanding all that it means, but I
know that my training has only just begun.*

*You will continue to teach me as long as I am willing to be your
student. As I leave the hallways of school buildings and go out into the
life You have prepared for me, help me to continue to embrace learning.
I pray that I will not resist your direction and your example. I pray that I
will grasp each lesson and hold on to it so that it will serve Your purpose
and keep me moving forward. You inspire my hopes and dreams, and I
pray to learn from You all the days of my life.*   Amen

Kindness

Kindness: It's More than a Random Act

We prove ourselves by our purity, our understanding, our patience, our **kindness**, *by the Holy Spirit within us, and by our sincere love.*

2 Corinthians 6:6 NLT

Have you ever committed a random act of kindness? You noticed someone needed a helping hand and so you stopped what you were doing to help them clean up a room or prepare a lunch for others without even thinking about it. Perhaps you were walking down the street, and when it started to rain, you gave your umbrella to an older lady ahead of you who didn't have one. You deliberately changed someone's day for the better. You helped them see the sunshine despite the rain or the clouds that had gathered around them.

Kindness is an important attribute that will serve you well as you go out into the world. You will notice, unfortunately, that some have forgotten that it's better to be kind. You will come up against the rude, and the crude, and the indifferent—those who have simply traded joy for bitterness and stony hearts. You probably went to school with a few people who were like that. Pitted against rudeness, kindness takes courage. You've got that.

As a believer, your job is to exhibit Christlike kindness to others. When you do, you instantly make a difference and you usher in the light that mitigates the darkness. Mother Teresa once shared this about kindness: "Spread love everywhere you go: First of all, in your own house. Let no one ever come to you without leaving better and happier. Be the living expression of God's kindness: kindness in your face, kindness in your eyes, kindness in your smile, kindness in your warm greeting."

Can you imagine what any environment you might find yourself in would be like, if we treated one another with such kindness? Opportunities abound for you to try to be the living expression of God's kindness.

That's not an easy task, but you've been created with a warm heart and a great smile, and God will bless you each time you turn your back on rudeness in favor of being kindhearted, compassionate, and gentle. It's a good day to sprinkle some kindness anywhere you happen to be. It doesn't have to be random; it can simply be who you are!

SHOWING KINDNESS

If there is any kindness I can show,
Or any good thing I can do to any human being,
Let me do it now, and not deter or neglect it,
As I shall not pass this way again.   William Penn

A HEART OF KINDNESS

Never let loyalty and kindness leave you!
Tie them around your neck as a reminder.
Write them deep within your heart.   Proverbs 3:3 NLT

SMILE

A smile is the universal language of kindness.   Author unknown

THREE RULES FOR A HAPPY LIFE

The first is to be kind.
The second is to be kind.
The third is to be kind.   Henry James

POOH'S LITTLE INSTRUCTION BOOK

Just because an animal is large, it doesn't mean he doesn't want kindness; however big Tigger seems to be, remember that he wants as much kindness as Roo.   A. A. Milne

THE GIFT OF KINDNESS

If your gift is to encourage others, be encouraging.
If it is giving, give generously.
If God has given you leadership ability, take the responsibility seriously.

And if you have a gift for showing kindness to others, do it gladly.

Romans 12:8 NLT

KIND WORDS

You can't speak a kind word too soon,
For you never know when it will be too late. Author unknown

Prayer

Dear Lord, I believe that the kindness of others has always helped me to be more trusting and more loving. The examples of teachers and parents and friends have served to show me what it means to be kind.

As I grow to understand more of what You would have me be in the world, I pray that one of those things is that I would be willing to be kind to others. It is not as easy as it sounds because little things sometimes get in the way, and most of those have to do with my ego. Let me not be too proud or arrogant or too driven by my goals that I cannot stop to offer simple kindness to people I meet along the way. I pray that I would be as willing to show kindness to others as You have been willing to show incredible kindness to me. Amen

Thankful

Thankful for the Little Things

*Keep your roots deep in him and have your lives built on him. Be strong in the faith, just as you were taught, and always be **thankful**.*

Colossians 2:7 NCV

As a graduate, you no doubt have gratitude for a lot of things that helped you get to the big day. You feel gratitude toward your teachers, who encouraged and inspired and helped you learn the things that you needed to know. You're grateful for your home and your family, the people who supported you and shared the ups and downs of school life, day to day. You may be thankful for your friends, who enriched the experience of growing up and in some way helped you learn more about yourself.

As a believer, you're also a person who realizes that all those things—teachers, family, and friends—come from the One who watches over your life and who wants good things for you. You are thankful for God's kindness to you and your gratitude for all He has done pleases Him. He loves to know that you are grateful for the efforts He makes on your behalf.

As you continue on your life path, you will discover that there are many things to give God credit for, things that make you thankful you have a relationship with Him. Some of those things are incidental, like sweet moments when someone noticed you and did something to draw you into a circle of friends, or the effort your family made to see you in a school play or go to a sporting event. Little things do mean a lot because most of your life will be created by small experiences that add up to immeasurable blessings.

The best thing you can do then is to stay close to Your Creator and show Him your appreciation by the way you live your life. Let Him see what you've learned from His discipline and His example—how you've grown because of His love.

It will serve you well your whole life to remember to let others know how thankful you are to share your days together. A thankful heart is a blessing to everyone.

HUMBLE THANKS

In ordinary life we hardly realize that we receive a great deal more than we give, and that it is only with gratitude that life becomes rich.

It is very easy to overestimate the importance of our own achievements in comparison with what we owe others.

Dietrich Bonhoeffer

THANKFUL THOUGHTS

Reflect upon your present blessings—
Of which every person has many—
Not on your past misfortunes,
Of which all people have some.

Charles Dickens

GRATEFUL TO BE YOU

There is always one thing
To be grateful for—
That you are yourself
And not somebody else.

Emily Dickinson

THANKFUL BY DEFINITION

Gratitude is from the same root word as grace—The boundless mercy of God.

Thanksgiving is from the same root word as think—So to think is to thank.

Willis P. King

REMEMBER TO GIVE THANKS

See that you do not forget what you were before, lest you take for granted the grace and mercy You received from God and forget to express Your gratitude each day.

Martin Luther

MOVING FORWARD

Let gratitude for the past inspire us with trust for the future.

François Fenélon

GIVE THANKS FOR EVERYTHING

Always give thanks to God the Father for everything, in the name of our Lord Jesus Christ.

Ephesians 5:20 NCV

Prayer

Dear Lord, I know I'm not always the first one to tell you I'm thankful for all You've done. I probably did not make it easy for You to try to guide me to the place I am today. Graduation is an important step for me, and I've given a lot of thought to what I want my life to be about. It's easy to do that when you've had a good balance of challenges and opportunities. My family has been so supportive of the things I hope to do and the dreams I've shared. I'm very thankful for them.

From now on, Lord, I'm going to try harder to share my appreciation for life and for good times and even hard times with You. I know that all together those things help me grow and become more of what You want me to be. I thank You right now for everything that helped me get to my Graduation Day and I look forward to what we will do together from here.

Amen

Faith

What Size Is Your Faith?

*Jesus answered, "I tell you the truth, if you have **faith** and do not doubt, you will be able to do what I did to this tree and even more. You will be able to say to this mountain, 'Go, fall into the sea.' And if you have faith, it will happen."*

Matthew 21:21 NCV

You may have completed one milestone at graduation, but you may wrestle with matters of faith most of your life. At times you will feel convicted by it enough to study and search and pray with confidence and trust in Jesus and all that God has done for you. Other times, you may wander a bit, doubting what you know because of the circumstances of your life or because of some new philosophy that you might choose to embrace. Safe to say, God wants you to remain strong in your faith and grow beyond any current understanding you may have.

As you encounter other thoughts and ideas, your belief system will be challenged. It may be mocked or ridiculed by strangers, or perhaps by friends and family as well. Part of the reason for this is that God calls each of us independently, apart from our families. The choice to serve Him must come from within our hearts in a way that shows we personally seek Him and long to live according to His will for us. It's that part of you that will walk in faith with God, building a relationship over time that will sustain you and help you endure whatever comes your way.

In the example from Matthew, the disciples were astonished when the fig tree simply withered at the command of Jesus. They wondered how such a thing could happen. They didn't understand that Jesus knew who He was in the Father and therefore He had no doubt about His authority. Your job from here is to discover more of who you are in the Father so that you can have faith that never succumbs to doubt, faith that can then ask anything of God.

It's a learning process, to be sure, and one that will bless you through-out your life. Go in faith and serve the Lord!

IN FAITH AND FAITHFULNESS

Teach me your way, Lord, that I may rely on your faithfulness;
give me an undivided heart, that I may fear your name.
I will praise you, Lord my God, with all my heart;
I will glorify your name forever.   Psalm 86:11–12 NIV

THE HANDLES OF FAITH

Every tomorrow has two handles. We can take hold of it by the
handle of anxiety, or by the handle of faith.   Author unknown

MOVING IN FAITH

Don't seek the faith that will move mountains. Seek the faith that
will move you!   Author unknown

HOPE, FAITH, LOVE

There is no love without hope,
No hope, without love,
And neither hope nor love without faith.   Saint Augustine

FAITH IN GOD

Say this to yourself. "I am loved by God more that I can either
conceive or understand." Let this fill all your soul and never leave
you. You will see that this is the way to find God.

                                                  Henri de Tourville

WHAT IS FAITH?

Faith is a living, busy, active, powerful thing; It is impossible for it
not to do us good continually.   Martin Luther

FAITH STEPS UP

When you get to the end of all the light you know, it's time to step
into the darkness of the unknown,

Faith is knowing that one of two things will happen:
Either you will be given something solid to stand on, or you will be taught how to fly.

Edward Teller

Prayer

Dear Lord, I feel like a novice when it comes to understanding what faith is or what it does, but I stand before You with a desire to learn more, to know what I need to see in order for faith to sustain me. I already know how easy it is to be drawn off into the world or into my own plans and simply neglect prayer and Bible reading and those things that keep me connected to You. I know that without Your help, every day, my faith will wither like that fig tree and I will be lost. I ask that You guard and protect me and continue to teach me what it really means to live as a Christian, to live as a person of faith. Thank You for loving me even more than I can understand.

Amen

Courage

Calling All Superheroes!

*Be alert. Continue strong in the faith. Have **courage**, and be strong.*

1 Corinthians 16:13 NCV

Many of us are fans of the superheroes who have found their way from comic book fame to the big screen. We love their amazing courage, their special skills that bring any fantasy to life, and the fact that they always show up in the nick of time. We may not be able to spin a spiderweb that lets us climb tall buildings, or fly through the air with a red cape, or turn into a flash of lightning, but we can still be a super kind of hero to someone.

You never know when the opportunity will present itself for you to be an instant hero. It may be the time you volunteer to read books to young children at the library, or when you offer to do a chore for your mom that gives her a few minutes for herself, or when you simply are there at the right time when someone needs a helping hand.

Perhaps you don't imagine that these "everyday" things take courage, but they often do. They put you outside your comfort zone or they ask you to give up your own free time.

As you move away from the neighborhood where you grew up and begin to find your own place in the world, the opportunity to muster your courage will come up many times.

Whether it's in facing new situations, meeting new people, or simply stepping up to do things for others you've never done before, you'll be glad to be a person of courage.

Dorothy Bernard said that "courage is fear that has said its prayers." As you continue to move forward, be sure to keep saying your prayers because Your Father in Heaven is a true superhero and He has great plans for your life. Be brave! Be strong! Have courage!

COURAGE STANDS UP OR SITS DOWN

Courage is what it takes to stand up and speak;
Courage is also what it takes to sit down and listen.

Author unknown

DEFINING COURAGE

Courage is the best gift of all;
Courage stands before everything.
It is what preserves our liberty, safety, life, and our homes and parents, our country and our children.
Courage comprises all things: A person with courage has every blessing.

Plautus

TWO KINDS OF COURAGE

It is curious that physical courage should be so common in the world, and moral courage so rare.

Mark Twain

FACING FEAR

Courage faces fear and thereby masters it.
Cowardice represses fear and is thereby mastered by it.

Martin Luther King Jr.

GOD IS WITH YOU

Be strong and brave. Don't be afraid of them and don't be frightened, because the Lord your God will go with you. He will not leave you or forget you.

Deuteronomy 31:6 NCV

COURAGE IS NUMBER ONE!

Courage is the first of human qualities because it is the quality which guarantees all the others.

Winston Churchill

BE COURAGEOUS!

Courage is the strength or choice to begin a change.
Determination is the persistence to continue in that change.

Author unknown

Prayer

Lord, I must admit that I don't give a lot of thought to the kind of courage I might need as I move away from the life I've known with friends and family, or as I begin to pursue my dreams in other places. I've always felt safe and strong because I knew other people had my back and would help me if I got into anything that was over my head.

I realize now that I need to trust You for everything that matters to me from here. I need Your help to be brave as I try new things and to be strong as I encounter obstacles that I've never dealt with before. I pray that I will always be close to You, drawing near You when I need guidance or help, or strength and courage. Help me to build my spiritual muscles so that I can face whatever is in front of me with confidence and joy.

Amen

Think

You've Graduated! Now It's Time to Think Again

*Finally, brothers and sisters, whatever is true, whatever is noble, whatever
is right, whatever is pure, whatever is lovely, whatever is admirable—if
anything is excellent or praiseworthy—**think** about such things. Whatever
you have learned or received or heard from me, or seen in me—put it into
practice. And the God of peace will be with you.* Philippians 4:8-9 NIV

You've certainly had a lot to think about as you prepared to celebrate your
graduation. You had to pass all the finals, get things in order to head into
the future, and even think about all that's been and all that is yet to be.

One of the great things about education is that it teaches you how to
think. It asks you to consider a variety of points of view and determine
your response to those views. It takes you down the path of researching
a topic so that you can think not only about the content of your research,
but also the process it takes to determine your results.

You've learned to do some critical thinking as you evaluated literature
or history or science. Those important skills will help you in all aspects of
your life as you move forward.

Sometimes, though, you create stories in your head that don't serve you
well. You find yourself being critical of your abilities or talents, wondering if you're ready to take on the world. You may not have all the support
you wish you would have to pursue your field of choice and so you doubt
yourself or others.

The best thing you can do when you're starting anything is not just to
think about it but to think twice about it. The more you review your opportunities, your ideas, and add them to the opinions of others, the more you
need to be able to think for yourself, and sometimes that means you have
to think again.

This Scripture from Philippians is a great place to start when you find yourself slipping into negative thoughts. It suggests that it is worthwhile to stop everything else and look at the positive things because those will be all around you. When you can clearly see that good things and beautiful things are available to you, it calms your thoughts and gives your heart and mind a sense of peace.

God would have you always look up and call on Him when you feel overwhelmed by thoughts that are spinning too quickly for you to grasp them. Give Him a chance to help you get off that crazy merry-go-round and calm your nerves. God cares about you and about everything you think. Just remember, you always have another think coming!

BE AWARE OF YOUR THOUGHTS

Watch your thoughts; they become words.
Watch your words; they become actions.
Watch your actions; they become habits.
Watch your habits; they become your character.
Watch your character; for it becomes your destiny.

Author unknown

THINKING AND BELIEVING

A Christian is a person who thinks in believing,
And who believes in thinking.   Saint Augustine

THINK AGAIN

Among mortals second thoughts are the wisest.   Euripides

THINK WITH YOUR HEART

A person may think their own ways are right, but the Lord weighs the heart.   Proverbs 21:2 NIV

FOOD FOR THOUGHT

Every thought is a seed.
If you plant crab apples, don't count on harvesting golden delicious.   Author unknown

RENEW YOUR MIND

Do not conform to the pattern of this world, but be transformed by the renewing of your mind. Then you will be able to test and approve what God's will is—his good, pleasing and perfect will.

Romans 12:2 NIV

Prayer

Dear Lord, thank You for giving me a strong heart and mind. Guard my thoughts from those who would deceive me or cause me to move away from You in some way. Help me when I am confused with choices I must make so that I am considerate of every option, thinking through each one with care. I know that sometimes I will not think about something I do, and even more, I may not stop to pray about it. I ask that You would nudge me a little and remind me that together we can work things out for my good.

Even though I'm a positive person, I know that I sometimes fall into negative thoughts when things don't go as I expected. I pray that I'll remember then to think on those things that strengthen my faith and help me to move past fear and confusion. Whatever I do, Lord, I pray that You will help me to be wise and to think twice about any action I intend to take. Guard my steps and my heart and mind. Amen

Integrity

Honesty Is Still the Best Policy

*"As for you, if you walk before me in **integrity** of heart and uprightness...*
and do all I command and observe my decrees and laws, I will establish
your royal throne over Israel forever."   1 Kings 9:4–5 NIV

Probably one of the best things you can ever do for yourself is to be honest and upright. That means you examine your motives and search your heart to discover what you should do in any given situation. You look for ways to approach God with nothing to hide. It makes an amazing difference in how you experience life.

It appears that integrity is not always the benchmark we might hope it would be. Our current culture allows for a lot of variations of truth, sometimes not even disguising the lies that it offers to those who are not discerning. When God spoke with David about establishing His heritage, creating a ruler from David's line forever, He wanted David's agreement that he would walk with God in honesty, committed to doing the things that David knew were right.

God wants the same thing from you. He wants to know that you won't betray His trust in you and simply choose to walk away, following the whims of the world and losing sight of all that He has given you.

Sometimes when someone wants to emphasize that they are telling the truth, they will add the phrase, "It's true, honest to God!"

Whatever you do, you'll find it's always best to be honest with God and with yourself. One of the people we remember in history is Abe Lincoln, a man who was often called "Honest Abe." Sadly, this is an accolade that few people will ever receive. Lincoln once stated, "I never had a policy. I have just tried to do my very best each and every day." Still it seems certain that Lincoln would aspire to "honesty is the best policy."

If you think honesty, integrity, truth, and uprightness are still your best policy, God will honor the work of your heart and hands and bless your life always. There's really nothing better than being able to hold your head up high, knowing that you have approached any aspect of life with integrity.

INTEGRITY AND KNOWLEDGE

Integrity without knowledge is weak and useless, and knowledge without integrity is dangerous and dreadful.   Samuel Johnson

BE TRUE TO YOURSELF

This above all: to thine own self be true,
And it must follow, as the night the day,
Thou canst not then be false to any man.   William Shakespeare

POPULARITY CONTEST

Truth is not always popular, but it is always right.

Author unknown

BE A BLESSING

Good people who live honest lives will be a blessing to their children.   Proverbs 20:7 NCV

GIVE INTEGRITY A CHANCE

Integrity: define it, deliver it, delight in it; create a place where it can be seen in everything you do.   K. Moore

STICK WITH THE TRUTH

Do not lie. Do not deceive one another.   Leviticus 19:11 NIV

Prayer

Lord, I fervently pray to live my life with integrity, honoring my family and doing the things that please You. Please help me to do that as I move out into the world. The hard part is that it's too easy sometimes to tell

a "white" lie or simply not share an honest thought, especially when I know it won't be accepted. It's not easy to stand up for things that I believe in even when I want to because I don't want to lose my friends.

I ask that You help me to have a heart that instantly reminds me when I've gone in the wrong direction or when I've been dishonest in any way. Help me to be truthful to myself so that I can more quickly get back on track if I've slipped away. Reveal to me any areas where I may not be as honest as I think I am so that I can work those things out with You and honor You with my whole heart and mind. Whatever else I do, I always want to be honest with You. Amen

Character

Will the Real You Please Stand Up!

Not only so, but we also glory in our sufferings, because we know that suffering produces perseverance; perseverance, **character***; and character, hope. And hope does not put us to shame, because God's love has been poured out into our hearts through the Holy Spirit, who has been given to us.*

Romans 5:3–5 NIV

As you move beyond graduation and continue on your life journey, one of the interesting discoveries you will make is in regard to your character. Up until now, you may have been called a "character" because of your charisma or your great sense of humor, but this definition goes way beyond that side of your personality.

Character is built on a foundation, much like you see in this description from Romans. It tells us that when we go through hard times, we're forced to endure and persevere. We have to continue to try and not give up. That aspect of personality that learns to push through the hard times and not quit is related to your character.

Your sense of integrity and pride come into play as you face the obstacles life brings. You find out just how willing you are to listen to God's guidance, just how much you're ready to stand up for the things you believe in, and more than that, you find out what it means to love others. People of good character watch out for others because their hearts are full of love and compassion.

Your strength of character then leads you to believe in the impossible, to hope in the things you simply cannot see and understand, and to keep going because you know with a certainty that God is with you. You know that because He led you from the start, through the whole maze that took you from difficulty to hope. He was there with you, shaping and molding and blessing your character.

You are getting to know who you really are and what kind of person you want to be. The more you can align your hopes and dreams with the ones Your Father in Heaven planned for you all along, the more you will become a person of great character.

Go out and show the world what it means to live with integrity and kindness, with faith and optimism, and you can be sure that God will be close to your side forever. Chances are good that He will think of you as one amazing character!

CREATING YOUR CHARACTER

Character is made by many acts;
But it may be lost by just a single one.   Author unknown

DEFINING CHARACTER

We never know how much one loves till we know how much one is willing to endure and suffer for us; and it is the suffering element that measures love. The characters that are great must be characters that are willing, patient, and strong enough to endure for others. To hold our nature in the service of another is divine and the greatest achievement of human character.

Adapted from Henry Ward Beecher

WHAT IS BEFORE US

What lies beyond us and what lies before us are tiny matters compared to what lies within us.   Ralph Waldo Emerson

A TEENAGER'S OBSERVATIONS

Parents can only give good advice or put children on the right paths, But the final framing of a person's character lies in their own hands.   Anne Frank

BECOMING YOU

Character cannot be developed in ease and quiet.
Only through experiences of trial and suffering can the soul be strengthened, the vision cleared, ambition inspired, and success achieved.   Helen Keller

A GOOD THOUGHT

Character is what you are in the dark.   Dwight L. Moody

PUT ME IN, COACH!

Be more concerned with your character than with your reputation, because your character is what you really are, while your reputation is merely what others think you are.   John Wooden

Prayer

Dear Lord, I pray to be a person of character. I don't know exactly what that means to me yet, but I know it is important and honorable. I pray that I will face the future with integrity, armed with Your love and Your Word, and when troubles fly all around me, that I would come up against them with confidence and character. Help me to understand what it means to be a person of good character in my friendships, my relationships with family and with significant others. Guide me to be a person of character in any work that I do, or tasks that I perform.

Thank You for giving me a family that instilled in me the qualities that help me to know what it means to be trustworthy and to have a strong moral and ethical code. These are some of the things I'm starting with as I leave school, and I'm praying that I will be wise in my choices, building good character as I go. Lord, I pray that I will make my family proud and that I will make You proud as well.   Amen

The Prayer of Saint Patrick

I rise today with the power of God to guide me,
The might of God to uphold me,
The wisdom of God to teach me,
The eye of God to watch over me,
The ear of God to hear me,
The word of God to give me speech,
The hand of God to protect me,
The path of God to lie before me,
The host of God to defend me
against the snares of the devil
and the temptations of the world,
Against everyone who meditates injury to me,
Whether far or near.
Amen

Family

Family Ties

*If any one does not provide for his relatives, and especially for his own
family, he has disowned the faith and is worse than an unbeliever.*

1 Timothy 5:8 RSV

The definition of family has grown to mean everything from those who
are your biological relatives to those who are your dearest friends in the
world. However you define it, there is nothing that means quite as much
as knowing you have people in your life who stick with you through the
good times and difficult times, who support you even when you are acting
a little bit crazy, and who continue to love you no matter what else is going
on. Your family ties are important, and they will help sustain you your
whole life.

Graduation may change your family dynamic, especially if you go off
to another city to work or for more education, but it won't change the fact
that you have a place to return, to seek good advice, and receive warm
hugs. Sure, you may wonder now and then how you got into a family like
yours, but you should know that your family is a gift of God, and that He
placed you in that family to nurture you and help you grow. After all, He
knew exactly what you would learn from them and how they would help
you develop into the person you are today. You needed them, and they
needed you. Always will. That's how it works.

The thing to keep in mind as you put on your backpack to leave home
is that these people will be praying for you, waiting for you, and loving you
no matter where you go in life. They will be seeking your good and hop-
ing for your best. They are your own personal cheering committee. Think
of them as your "True North, or your North Star." You can look up to the
heavens and know that God has given you this family as a compass point,
a place you can go back to whenever you need them.

Desmond Tutu once wrote, "You don't choose your family. They are

God's gift to you, as you are to them." Carry your family in your heart wherever you go from here.

Blessed be the ties that bind you to your family!

FAMILY TIES

His name is the Lord—rejoice in his presence!
Father to the fatherless, defender of widows—
This is God, whose dwelling is holy. God places the lonely in families.

Psalm 68:4–6 NIV

FAMILY EDUCATION

The mind of Christ is to be learned in the family. Strength of character may be acquired at work, but beauty of character is learned at home. There the affections are trained.

Henry Drummond

FAMILY IS A PRIORITY

The family was ordained by God before He established any other institution, even before He established the church.   Billy Graham

SUSTAINABLE FAMILIES

Family life is too intimate to be preserved by the spirit of justice. It can be sustained by a spirit of love which goes beyond justice.

Reinhold Niebuhr

FAMILY DIFFERENCES

God is the first object of our love: Its next office is to bear the defects of others. And we should begin the practice of this amid our own household.

John Wesley

RAISE UP A CHILD

The family should be a place where each new human being can have an early atmosphere conducive to the development of constructive creativity.

Edith Schaeffer

Prayer

Dear Lord, I am grateful and humbled that You gave me such a wonderful family. I know that I am blessed because no matter what I may do, I trust that these people are in my corner, the champions of all I hope to be. I know we are not a perfect family by any means, but we have learned how to get along despite our petty differences. We've learned to pray and to share and to communicate and to help each other.

I know that what I learned in my upbringing and in my home life will help me no matter what I choose to do because I know what it means to have support and loyalty. More than that, I know that You are watching out for me and for my family, and so whether we are together or apart, we can count on Your love and grace and mercy to sustain us. Bless my family with each new day. Amen

Friend

A Good Friend Is Awesome!

A friend is always loyal, and a brother is born to help in time of need.

Proverbs 17:17 NIV

One of the best parts of being in school is that it gives you the opportunity to discover those people that you genuinely can call "friend." There may be no other environment that provides a testing ground for friendship like the one you've just been through because you have had a chance to experience what it is to be a friend, and how much it means to have a friend.

As you look back on your school years, you will remember those people who shaped your thinking about concepts such as loyalty, character, and kindness. As you grow from here, you will take some of these important lessons and utilize them with people you don't know right now but who may become lifelong friends.

Beyond the blessing of the friends you make at school and over your lifetime is the genuine understanding you will have of what it means to be a "friend" of God. The characteristics you appreciate in people you know and love are the same ones that sustain your relationship with Your Creator. In Christ you have a friend who never changes, doesn't get tired of you, doesn't get jealous or moody, but simply loves you as you are. The friendship you have with Jesus means you have someone to talk to anytime, to confess your worries and your heartaches to, and to share your faith with. It is through your friendship with God that you learn the most about what to look for in a real friend here on earth.

As you go on to make new friends, be sure to consider those attributes that are healthy and wholesome, the ones that encourage your heart and mind in positive ways and bring you joy every time you think of them. Friendship comes with high standards, and Jesus set the bar for you, so you could understand what it takes to be a good friend and to have a good friend.

May you engage with loving and generous friends wherever you go and may one or two stick with you for a lifetime, becoming closer than a brother.

YOU ARE MY FRIEND

[Jesus:] "You are my friends if you obey me."   John 15:14 NIV

THE TIMING OF FRIENDSHIP

Sometimes being a friend is mastering the art of timing:

There is a time for silence, a time to let go and allow people to hurl themselves into their own destiny.

And a time to prepare to pick up the pieces when it's all over.

Octavia Butler

WALK WITH ME

Don't walk behind me, I may not lead.
Don't walk in front of me, I may not follow.
Just walk beside me and be my friend.   Albert Camus

TO BE A GOOD FRIEND

To have a good friend is one of the highest delights of life;
To be a good friend is one of the noblest and most difficult
undertakings.   Author unknown

YOU, TOO?

Friendship is born at that moment when one person says to another: "What? You too? I thought I was the only one."

C. S. Lewis

KEEPING THE LIGHT ON

Sometimes our light goes out but is blown into flame by another human being. Each of us owes deepest thanks to those who have rekindled this light.   Albert Schweitzer

WHAT GOOD FRIENDS DO

My friends have made the story of my life. In a thousand ways they have turned my limitations into beautiful privileges, and enabled me to walk serene and happy in the shadow cast by my deprivation.

Helen Keller

A REAL FRIEND

A real friend is the one who walks in when the rest of the world walks out.

Walter Winchell

Prayer

Dear Lord, I am just beginning to understand the gift of real friendships. I've been blessed to have friendships within my family and with people that I've known from school. I pray that I would learn to be a really good friend to the people You put in my life. These school years have shown me that it isn't always easy to be a real friend who builds others up and puts others first.

Help me to find those people who truly know how to be a friend, the ones that You know will stand by me when I'm overwhelmed by challenges, and who will celebrate with me when something good has come my way. I pray, too, that You will walk beside me and remind me that I truly do have a friend in Jesus. Let me never neglect to build my relationship with You.

Amen

Tomorrow

What Will Tomorrow Bring?

Do not boast about **tomorrow**, *for you do not know what a day may bring forth.*   Proverbs 27:1 NIV

Now that you've graduated, it's likely that you are turning your thoughts and your focus toward tomorrow and the future. You're probably excited to get things moving so you can begin your new life adventures. It's good to face tomorrow with a positive outlook, goals in place, and desires of your heart somewhat established. No doubt, some of your interests will change over the next few years, but you have a place to start.

This Proverb is a reminder that we can look toward tomorrow, but we always have to get through today first. What that means is that you have more opportunity to make today count than you have the chance to figure out all that might happen tomorrow. Perhaps each today lived well means that you could get a better tomorrow.

The good news is that God is with you today, tomorrow, and always. He alone knows what tomorrow may bring, and as the saying goes, "I may not know what tomorrow holds, but I know who holds tomorrow." Since tomorrow then is totally in God's hands, you can embrace today with gusto.

Perhaps you still have thank-you notes to write from your graduation celebration. Maybe you have to create a priority list of things you need to accomplish before you are ready to move away from home. Today is the day to deal with practical matters and continue to seek God's advice and counsel on future matters.

With great intention, take today, and live it with joy and faithfulness, walking with God in all you do, and He will continue to work out the details of all your tomorrows. This is the day the Lord has made, so take it on, laugh out loud, and celebrate your blessings!

A BRIGHT FUTURE

The future is as bright as the promises of God.

Adoniram Judson

COUNTING THE MOMENTS

The next moment is as much beyond our grasp, and as much in God's care, as that a hundred years away. Care for the next minute is just as foolish as care for a day in the next thousand years. In neither can we do anything, in both God is doing everything.

C. S. Lewis

LIVING FOR TODAY

Even if I knew that tomorrow the world would go to pieces, I would still plant my apple tree.

Martin Luther

THE FUTURE

The future belongs to those who believe in the beauty of their dreams.

Eleanor Roosevelt

DON'T WORRY ABOUT TOMORROW

Do not worry about tomorrow, for tomorrow will worry about itself.

Matthew 6:34 NIV

THE UNKNOWN

Never be afraid to trust an unknown future to a known God.

Corrie ten Boom

ASSURANCE

I know not what the future hath
Of marvel and surprise;
Assured of this, that life and earth
His mercy underlies.

John Greenleaf Whittier

Prayer

Father in Heaven, thank You for continually assuring me that You are with me and that I can freely live today in Your grace, knowing we will work out the future together. Whatever details I need to know, whatever part I need to play in securing the future You have for me, then I pray I would be wise and play my part well. I ask that You would nudge me when I am getting away from the plan You have designed, softening my heart so I am willing to listen.

I'm not sure what tomorrow might bring, but I surrender today to You, asking that your protection and guidance would lead me forward. Strengthen me when I am feeling weak or lazy or simply giving in to my own stubbornness.

I pray that I will please you with my hopes and dreams as I lay them at the foot of the cross, waiting for Your direction to move into each new day. Thank you for loving me so much today that You will keep molding me and shaping me to become all I'm meant to be in the future.   Amen

Worry

Graduating from Worry

*Do not **worry** about your life, what you will eat or drink, Or about your body, what you will wear.*   Matthew 6:25 NIV

It appears that each of us has a kind of "worry" personality. We either worry about absolutely everything, wondering how the details of our lives will ever get worked out, or we go from day to day, seemingly disconnected to all the personal dramas and not really worrying about anything. Whether you worry a little or a lot, the idea that Jesus would have you recall is that you truly don't have to, nor should you, worry about a thing. Even though worrying may seem like a natural response to our troubles, it's actually contrary to our faith. Faith asserts that we trust God to take care of us and that we believe He is connected to the details of our lives. If that is truly the case, then faith should trump worry.

If you're the kind of person who spent most of the time during your final exams worrying about whether you'd graduate, you might want to check in with your heart and evaluate where you stand in your faith. If you're willing, you can hand your worries over to God and let Him take care of each and every one. After all, that is His job!

As it happens, most of the time you worry about things that are either not in your control at all or won't ever occur anyway. Mark Twain once said, "I am an old man and have known a great many troubles, but most of them have never happened."

When you find yourself getting overanxious or you're suffering with a sleepless night, then maybe it's time to graduate from worry, and simply let God take care of things. Take a deep breath, pray, and put all those concerns of your heart in front of Him, and settle back to go to sleep. God will watch over you and He'll take all those worries on to Himself. He's up all night anyway.

May God bless you and keep you far from the path of worry.

GIVE GOD YOUR WORRIES

Give all your worries and cares to God, for he cares about what happens to you.

1 Peter 5:7 NIV

COME BACK DOWN TO EARTH

If you believe that feeling badly or worrying long enough will change a past or future event, then you are residing on another planet with a different reality system.

Author unknown

THINGS WILL WORK OUT

I believe God is managing affairs and that He doesn't need any advice from me. With God in charge, I believe everything will work out for the best in the end.

So what is there to worry about?

Henry Ford

A LITTLE STORY FOR YOU

A man ninety years old was asked to what he attributed his longevity.

"I reckon," he said, with a twinkle in his eye, "it's because most nights I went to bed and slept when I should have sat up and worried."

Dorothea Kent

MARTIN LUTHER'S CHAT WITH BIRDS

"Good morning, theologians! You wake up and sing. But I, old fool, know less than you and worry about everything, instead of simply trusting in the Heavenly Father's care."

PEACE, PLEASE!

Oh, how great peace and quietness would the person possess who should cut off all vain anxiety and place all confidence in God.

Thomas à Kempis

THE CURE FOR WORRY

Anxiety is the rust of life, destroying its brightness and weakening its power.

A childlike and abiding trust in Providence is its best preventative and cure.

Author unknown

Prayer

Lord, I will readily admit that I worry more than I should. So many things add to my anxiety level, and before I know it, I'm locked into the drama and worrying about what to expect. So far, it doesn't appear that the worrying has had much benefit apart from giving me something to do.

It has occurred to me that if I really want to let go of all my anxiety, the better thing might be to simply come to you in prayer. That gives me something to do that is productive and helpful. Certainly, our prayer times give me a chance to bare my soul and tell You all that I'm feeling and thinking. Help me to try not to hide from You when I'm nervous or worried about something that is going on in my life. Help me instead to give my spinning mind a rest and sit down with You. Help me to simply be still in Your presence until I feel calm again.

I ask Your forgiveness for those times that I hold on to worry more tightly than I hold on to my faith. I pray that I will remember You are always ready to help me with anything that is going on. Thank You for Your love and kindness.

Amen

Laughter

Laughter Is Good for the Soul

*He will yet fill your mouth with **laughter** and your lips with shouts of joy.*
Job 8:21 NIV

One of the healthiest things you can do each day is to have a good laugh. You know, the kind where tears are rolling down your cheeks, you're nearly doubled over with delight, and you cannot contain yourself no matter what you do. Laughter has taken over your heart, mind, and soul. What a relief it is and what fun to share with people you love!

Former United States President Dwight D. Eisenhower had this important message about laughter. He said, "Laughter can relieve tension, soothe the pain of disappointment, and strengthen the spirit for the formidable tasks that always lie ahead."

Now that you've graduated, you have a lot of important tasks ahead of you. Some you know all about, and others will come along to challenge your thoughts and inspire your direction. In God's Providence, you don't need to look ahead with anxiety, or concern yourself about every detail of any event you may have planned. You simply have to remember that you're in good hands, and that you can rest in that assurance.

When your heart is at peace, you can make little moments count, sharing time with friends, laughing over inside jokes, enjoying the best of what is behind you. Laughter will open the door to future friendships because you will anticipate enjoying even more good times as you grow and move forward.

If you've been struggling with your ability to calm your nerves as you prepare for all that is ahead of you, see if you can take some time out, watch a great comedy movie, or get with friends and simply enjoy the gift of laughter. It will serve you well, and before you know it, your anxiety will disappear.

May God grant you a merry heart and lots of reasons to laugh right out loud!

LAUGHING TOGETHER

Laughter is the shortest distance between two people.

Victor Borge

SUNNY SIDE UP

Always laugh when you can; it is cheap medicine.
Merriment is a philosophy not well understood. It is the sunny side of existence.

Lord Byron

THANKFUL FOR A LAUGH

Of all the things God created, I am often most grateful He created laughter.

Chuck Swindoll

ALL THE MORE REASON TO LAUGH

Humor is the great thing, the saving thing. The minute it crops up, all our irritations and resentments slip away and a sunny spirit takes their place.

Mark Twain

LAUGHTER IS CONTAGIOUS

A smile is a lovely thing,
A giggle brings delight,
But when something strikes you funny
Only one thing feels quite right.
It starts its way up from your toes
Then claps your hands
As on it goes, all the way up to your nose.
You make a squeal, you just can't hide
That doubles you from side to side,
Inviting nearly everyone
To slap their knees and join the fun.
For now, there's nothing to be done;
The room is filled with laughter!

K. Moore

Prayer

Dear God, there's nothing more wonderful than being able to laugh right out loud with great bursts of joy and enthusiasm. I've loved laughing with my friends over the years and sharing moments that have become warm memories. I pray that You will bless me with many opportunities for tear-filled laughter, the kind that is contagious and full of the spirit of life. I pray that this kind of laughter would bring healing to awkward moments, and balance to challenging ones.

Help me, Lord, to recognize in others a need to have more spontaneous joy, more reasons to laugh. Bless those I love with happiness and opportunities to share incredible times of great, unbridled joy. You are the author of love and laughter, and I thank You for giving this generous form of love to me and the people around me.

Amen

Heart

Follow Your Heart

*Above all else, guard your **heart**, for everything you do flows from it.*

Proverbs 4:23 NIV

Probably one of your greatest teachers in life is your heart. It grieves when you're troubled or sad over the loss of a friendship. It motivates you to celebrate when something wonderful happens and it raises your spirits. The author of Proverbs wisely suggests that you guard your heart, protect it, and watch over the things you allow it to take in. Why? Because the actions, the choices, the decisions you make throughout your life will often be decisions you make with your heart.

You may have already discovered that the world is not a protective parent. It will not pay any attention to what happens to your heart—only God can do that, as you put your life in God's hands. Jesus reminded you to love God with your whole heart, with your soul, and with your mind.

Imagine what it means to love God with your whole heart. It may mean that you can't stop talking about Him. You can't help wanting to spend time with God because you miss Him when you're off doing other things. It may mean that you talk with Him all through the day and that when you have difficult choices to make, you put your thoughts and ideas before Him and ask for His guidance. It also means that you tell Him how wonderful He is and how much you appreciate the amazing number of blessings He has bestowed upon you. Isn't that what love does?

If your heart is in the right place, meaning that it is centered on discovering more and more of what it means to love God, then you are always going to move in the right direction. You will be able to trust and follow your heart. When you invited Jesus into your heart, He came to live with you, so that together you can accomplish the purposes for which you were born.

It's time for you to step out into the world, set new goals, create new dreams, and be inspired by the love in your heart. As it says in 1 Chronicles 28:9, "For the Lord sees every heart and understands and knows every plan and thought. If you seek him, you will find him."

As the Lord leads, follow your heart and love Him with all you've got!

YOUR HEART AND YOUR HEAD

To handle yourself, use your head. To handle others, use your heart.

Author unknown

A WORD TO THE WISE

See that your primary focus is about your heart:
That there God's image may be planted,
That there God's interests may be advanced,
That there the world and temptations are subdued,
That there the love of sin is cast out,
That there, in your heart, the desire for holiness grows.

Adapted from Jonathan Edwards

WHAT IS ESSENTIAL

It is only with the heart that one can see rightly. What is essential is invisible to the eye.

Antoine de Saint-Exupéry

AN OPEN HEART

Neither prayer, nor praise, nor the hearing of the Word will be profitable to those who have left their hearts behind them.

C. H. Spurgeon

WHAT CAN YOU GIVE HIM?

What can I give Him, Poor as I am?
If I were a shepherd, I would bring a lamb.
If I were a Wise Man, I would do my part—
Yet what can I give Him? Give my heart!

Christina Rossetti

WHEN YOUR HEART SPEAKS

Good people have good things in their hearts, and so they say good things.

Matthew 12:35 NCV

Prayer

Dear Lord, it is my hope and desire to put my heart in order. I pray that you would give me a clean heart, a right heart, a heart that is truly open to Your leading and Your purposes. I ask that You melt my heart when I'm being stubborn or I'm not willing to listen to You or to others who would guide me along the right paths of life.

Protect my heart when I am innocent or unaware of the agenda others may have that could do me any kind of harm. Challenge my heart when I need to be reminded of who I am or all that I hope to be. Forgive me when I simply walk away from You and choose to walk on alone. You knocked on the door of my heart, and ever since I answered that door, I've been learning what it means to follow You and to follow my heart. I thank You for being with me now and blessing all that is yet ahead of me.

Amen

Life

The Meaning of Your Life

A thief comes to steal and kill and destroy, but I came to give life—life in all its fullness.   John 10:10 NCV

The pundits abound with ideas about the meaning of life. It's an age-old question and the only one who can truly define it is you. No matter what existential philosophy you may encounter to try to answer the question, the better question may be, "What is the meaning of your life?" The Creator of this universe and the thousands that exist outside planet Earth would have you seek that answer, for He designed you with a very special purpose in mind. He knew you would come along and so He joyfully anticipates all that you will do from here.

Ever since God breathed life into the first man, Adam, He's been breathing His Spirit into human beings, knowing that some would disregard His gifts, some would embrace them, and many would rest somewhere in the middle, never quite doing either one.

Is life all about you? Perhaps for the months prior to your graduation, it seemed like it was. Everyone rallied around you, offering support as you finished the tasks of final exams and created plans for the future. You were in the spotlight, enjoying the fun of loving attention.

As you go out on your own, though, you will quickly notice that the spotlight is off, the adoring crowds are gone, and you have to figure out what life means to you from here. You have to determine which way you will go. Will you disregard all that God has done, or will you embrace His love and guidance, or simply put your thoughts on hold when it comes to God's purposes for your life?

These are the choices in front of you. These are the choices that will ultimately inform you as to the meaning of your life. You have a lot to do and a lot to give, and God knows the amazing plans He has for you.

May you embrace your new life with compassion for others, excitement for all that is ahead, and with a heart that looks to know more of all that God has for you. Remember, then, your life is God's gift to you; what you do with it is your gift to God!

THE BOOK OF LIFE

In the book of life, the answers are not in the back.

Charlie Brown (Charles Schulz)

LIFE IS AN EDUCATION

Life is not a holiday, but an education. The one eternal lesson for us all is how better we can love.

Henry Drummond

MAKING A LIFE

We make a living by what we get. We make a life by what we give.

Martin Luther King Jr.

LIFE STUDY

The unexamined life is not worth living.

Socrates

A LIFE OF FAITH

Order your soul, reduce your wants;
Live in charity, associate in Christian community;
Obey the laws; trust in Providence.

Saint Augustine

TO HAVE A BLESSED LIFE

There is no more blessed way of living, than the life of faith upon a covenant-keeping God—To know that we have no care, for He cares for us; that we have no need of fear, except to fear Him; that we need have no troubles, because we cast our burdens on the Lord, and are conscious that He will sustain us.

C. H. Spurgeon

YOUR LIFE, YOUR GIFTS

There are different kinds of spiritual gifts, but they all come from the same Spirit. There are different ways to serve the same Lord, and we can each do different things. Yet the same God works in all of us and helps us in everything we do.   1 Corinthians 12:4–6 CEV

SHARING YOUR GIFTS

When I stand before God at the end of my life, I would hope that I would not have a single bit of talent left and could say, "I used everything You gave me."   Erma Bombeck

Prayer

Dear Lord, I'm really just getting started at this thing called life. I've lived within the community of my church and my family and my friends. Now I'm going to learn more about myself, more about the gifts and talents You've given me and the best ways I can use them. It's a little bit scary to step out into the world, but I know that You will be with me, helping me to make good choices, and showing me more of what You would have me do. I pray that I would serve you well and that I would always remember that life is sacred, and that You designed each of us to do a special work. I know I have a lot to learn, but I'm ready to give this amazing thing called life every chance it deserves. Help me, then, to lean on You for all I do from here.   Amen

Grace

Living in Grace for a Lifetime

*And God is able to make all **grace** abound to you, So that in all things at all times, having all that you need, you will abound in every good work.*

2 Corinthians 9:8 NIV

Maybe you think that getting to your Graduation Day was an experience of amazing grace. After all, you worked hard, but there were more than a few uncertain moments. It's helpful to grasp the concept of living in grace because that's where you've been living since the day you were born. Grace as it comes to you from God has a very special meaning. It is something that God does for you despite anything you have done or will ever do. Grace is what we receive from God even when we don't deserve it, and mercy is when God lovingly does not give us what we do deserve. You live now, and will forever live, in God's grace and mercy.

As you walk out into the world, think of God's grace as the air you breathe. His grace allows you to live your life, make mistakes, fall down and get up, and still be loved. His grace looks to discover what motivates your actions and then brings forgiveness when your actions offend God. God's grace is steadfast and is not something you can earn. He has freely given it to you.

When you remember how much grace, forgiveness, renewal, and possibility God has given you, you're better able to extend grace to others. When you're tempted to judge someone else, you might reconsider and say something like, "There but by the grace of God go I." That means you know that you have been blessed beyond measure, beyond what you deserve because God is love and He has mercy on you.

Sometimes we call the prayer we say before a meal "grace." Perhaps that simple act, that thought, will keep your heart and mind in Christ Jesus. Let it help you recall for the rest of your life that you live and breathe in the grace of God each day. May God's grace abound in your life forever!

THE WILL OF GOD

Where the will of God leads you, the grace of God will keep you.

Author unknown

YOU NEED GOD'S GRACE

Nothing whatever pertaining to godliness and real holiness can be accomplished without grace.

Saint Augustine

THE TREASURE

Cheap grace is grace without discipleship,
Grace without the cross, grace without Jesus Christ,
Living and incarnate.
Costly grace is the treasure hidden in the field;
For the sake of it a person will gladly go
And sell all that he has to attain it.

Dietrich Bonhoeffer

YOUR BEST DAYS, YOUR WORST DAYS

Your worst days are never so bad that you are beyond the reach of God's grace.

And your best days are never so good that you are beyond the need of God's grace.

Jerry Bridges

WORTH PONDERING

Heaven goes by favor. If it were by merit, you would stay out and your dog would go in.

Mark Twain

MY GRACE IS SUFFICIENT

But he said to me, "My grace is enough for you. When you are weak, my power is made perfect in you." So I am very happy to brag about my weaknesses. Then Christ's power can live in me.

2 Corinthians 12:9 NCV

JOAN OF ARC'S PRAYER

If I am not in a state of grace, God bring me there;
If I am, God keep me there. Amen

Prayer

Gracious Lord, I grew up singing "Amazing Grace," and even though I've always known the words, the understanding of what it means to live in Your unending grace is still a mystery to me. I am certain that grace is what sustains me when I'm ready to go off on my own, thinking I know better than anyone else what I need to do next. I am humbled that grace brings me back again, reminding me how loved I am despite my moods or my sinfulness. You have always blessed me with Your favor in the sense that You do not let me get too far from Your side.

I pray, Lord, that as I go out from my friends and family, I will continue to live in Your abundant grace and mercy. Help me to see Your hand at work in my life whether I'm reading a book, talking with friends, or walking through the woods. Help me to understand that You have freely given this grace to me so that I can spend my life learning more about You. Thank You for giving me the grace to graduate and prepare for a new life ahead.

Amen

Study

No More Study Halls!

Always remember what is written in the Book of the Teachings. **Study** *it day and night to be sure to obey everything that is written there. If you do this, you will be wise and successful in everything.*

Joshua 1:8 NCV

Just because you graduated, you haven't left studying behind. It may not be the formal kind of study you do in school, but you will still have a lot of opportunity to engage your study skills as you go on with your life.

When Joshua was leading the children of Israel, he reminded them that it was important for them to be in the Word, in the teachings that they had at the time. He suggested that they study day and night—in other words, all the time. He didn't want them to forget anything that God had already told them because their lives depended on their willingness to obey God's commands. He promised them that if they studied, their reward would be that they would be wiser, and they would be successful in everything they did.

That's a pretty hefty promise and it's one that is true for you as well. God wants you to continue in the Word for the rest of your life. He'd like you to make it a priority, perhaps doing morning devotions and evening prayers. However you choose to do it, the fact is that the more you know about God, the better your relationship will be. The more you know one another, the more God can bless your life.

It's always going to be important for you to study, meditate, train, learn, do all you can to build on the foundation of what you understand about God. Getting into a great Bible study group may be one way to continue your education. Spending one-on-one time with God every day is another way to do so. The more you spend time with Him, the more you will recognize His voice when you are seeking guidance and direction. You may not have any study halls now, but you still have lots of time to focus your heart and mind on the subject, essence, presence, and will of God. This will be a lifelong tutoring opportunity.

STUDY TO BE HAPPY

But the truly happy people are those who carefully study God's perfect law that makes people free, and they continue to study it. They do not forget what they heard, but they obey what God's teaching says. Those who do this will be made happy.

James 1:25 NCV

AN APPETITE FOR BOOKS

Some books are to be tasted, others to be swallowed, and some few to be chewed and digested. Francis Bacon

CAN'T STUDY TODAY

One of my great regrets is that I have not studied enough. I wish I had studied more and preached less. Billy Graham

BIBLE STUDY

It should fill the memory, rule the heart, and guide the feet.

Author unknown

YOU CAN'T OUTGROW YOUR BIBLE

Nobody ever outgrows Scripture; the book widens and deepens with our years. C. H. Spurgeon

THE LIVING WORD

God did not write a book and send it to a messenger to be read at a distance by unaided minds.

He spoke a Book and lives in His spoken words, constantly speaking His words and causing the power of them to persist across the years. A. W. Tozer

THE THREE STAGES OF BIBLE STUDY

The Cod Liver Stage: You take it like medicine.
The Shredded Wheat Stage: It's nourishing, but dry.
The Peaches and Cream Stage: It's consumed with passion and
pleasure.

Author unknown

Prayer

*Dear Lord, I must confess that I am not a big fan of studying. I always
liked having a study hall in school because it meant I could get my
homework done and not have to think about it after school was over for
the day. I studied for tests when I had to, but I never thought being able
to study was much fun. I need your help as I leave formal school days
behind to get into a studying mind-set. I know that I have a lot of reading
to do in my Bible to get a clear understanding of what You might expect
from me and what You want me to know.*

*You've already helped me so much by giving me a basic
understanding that You want to be part of my life forever. You've blessed
me with a sense that Jesus is real and that I can continue to build our
relationship. Since reading the Bible is part of the way I can study
more about You and Jesus, then please inspire my heart and mind as
I go forward. Protect me from the philosophers and the intellectuals
who might want to derail my faith. Motivate me to stay close to You in
all I do.*

Amen

Victory

Moving Beyond Your Diploma

In fact, this is love for God: to keep his commands. And his commands are not burdensome, for everyone born of God overcomes the world. This is the victory that has overcome the world, even our faith. 1 John 5:3–4 NIV

Everyone loves to win. We love to see our team push through impossible odds and come out victorious. We love to get behind a champion and cheer until the gold medal is attained. Nothing gives us quite the same satisfaction as going after a goal and finally winning the day.

You just went through that kind of victory at your graduation. You worked hard, set the course, kept going even when things were tough, and came out with that diploma in your hand . . . victory! Enjoy the celebration and tuck the memory of cheers into your heart so they can move with you into the world.

Once you leave your school days behind, it's still important to set goals, work through challenges, and even find those who might champion your efforts. It's always good to have someone in your corner. You'll always have the love and support of your family and friends, but as you move on, you'll have a more Divine resource as well. Since you chose to follow Jesus, He will go with you. He has overcome the world and has already attained the victory. He knows what it feels like to celebrate a big win.

Help Him continue the celebration by lifting His banner high and letting others know all that He has done for you. He is the one who will be your champion from now on, helping you through the setbacks, and applauding your victories.

Your well-earned diploma will give you new opportunities, connect you with new friends, and inspire your life direction. Your faith will be the door that keeps you strong, content in the ups and downs, and able to persevere no matter what the odds of winning may be. With Jesus, your ultimate victory is already won. He is forever by your side.

Congratulations on all you've done to get to your Graduation Day. God bless you and keep you from here.

THE VICTORY CLIMB

The road to success runs uphill. Don't expect to break any speed records.

Author unknown

KING OF THE MOUNTAIN

The man on top of the mountain did not fall there.

Author unknown

OVERCOMING OBSTACLES

The secret of success for real champions and winners in this world is not about their natural aptitude and talent.

Victory comes from their ability to overcome obstacles, including the obstacles they place in their own paths.

That's what makes a difference between victory and loss.

Author unknown

THE DIPLOMA

A sheepskin is a blessing,
So artfully scrolled—
Your name in perfect letters
Beautiful and bold.
It speaks of past achievement
And of victory today,
And ushers in the future
Where Jesus leads the way.

K. Moore

OPTIMISM BRINGS VICTORY

Optimism is the faith that leads to achievement. Nothing can be done without hope and confidence.

Helen Keller

YOU CAN'T HAVE A VICTORY WITHOUT A TARGET

The truest difference between success and failure, between the strong and the weak, between the big and the small, is nothing but a powerful aim in life, a purpose fixed toward victory...do or die. No perfect speech or manners, no culture or education, no pull or influence, can make a difference in this world without it.

Aim high!   Author unknown

THE ULTIMATE VICTORY

But thanks be to God! He gives us the victory through our Lord Jesus Christ.   1 Corinthians 15:57 NIV

Prayer

Father in Heaven, I am grateful for achieving my goal, of getting a diploma. I believe that this one action will make a big difference in the opportunities that are yet ahead of me. I worked hard and learned the things I needed to know to get to this day, and I believe I will be blessed beyond measure. You have been an important part of my journey, the One I could turn to when things were not going well, or when I simply couldn't stay on track. You inspired my thinking and guided me to the teachers and friends and family members who made a difference.

I'm grateful that I don't have to live in this world totally on my own, but that I have many people around me who care for me and serve as examples of how I can do something better. I know that I have achieved this diploma through a lot of effort and a lot of trial and error. It's important for me to tell You that I truly believe I could not have done it without You. Thank You for your inspiration, Your steadfast faith in me, and Your continual love.   Amen

God's Promises

YOU: It's impossible!
GOD: **All things are possible with me.**

YOU: I'm too tired!
GOD: **I will give you rest.**

YOU: Nobody really loves me.
GOD: **I love you.**

YOU: I can't do anything more.
GOD: **My grace is sufficient for you.**

YOU: I can't forgive myself.
GOD: **I forgive you.**

YOU: I'm afraid!
GOD: **I have not given you a spirit of fear.**

YOU: I'm just so worried and frustrated!
GOD: **Cast all your burdens on Me.**

YOU: I'm not smart enough!
GOD: **I give you wisdom.**

YOU: I feel all alone.
GOD: **I will never leave you nor forsake you.**

Acknowledgments

Even though it's been some time since my own graduation from high school and college, I still remember the mixture of joy and anxiety that came with the diploma. After all, the protective covering that I received from my parents was going to come off and I would have to learn to navigate the world on my own. It's been an amazing journey since those days, but I will always be grateful to my parents, Douglas and Beverly Moore, who gave me the proverbial roots and wings.

I also am grateful for my alma mater, Unatego Central School, in upstate New York, for providing the foundation I needed to move forward and for honoring me with induction into their Hall of Distinction in January of 2018.

I dedicate this book to all those students who will graduate from high schools and colleges in the coming years, grateful that the future will be in your hands, guided by God's love and mercy. In that regard, I especially dedicate this book to my two granddaughters approaching graduation: Avery Lucille Gurney, who is sure to be a rising star in whatever field she pursues; and Anika Casanova, who will brighten the future for all of us.

I'm grateful to my husband, Bruce Barbour, for inspiring the whole idea for the series of What a Great Word! books and who inspires my life every day as he walks faithfully with God.

Finally, I thank Hachette Book Group, especially Rolf Zettersten and Keren Baltzer for catching the vision for this series; and to my copyeditor who did an amazing job, Joan Matthews. May God continue to bless the work of your hands.

What a Great Word for Grads
Alphabetical List

About the Author

KAREN MOORE is the best-selling author of more than 100 books for kids, teens, and adults with her inspirational daily devotionals. Karen teaches at writing conferences and is a keynote speaker for conference events and women's groups. She has also worked in the greeting card industry, creating thousands of greeting cards, as a product development specialist, and she's also worked as a book publisher. Currently, Karen is working on two licensed properties for children. She is married and makes her home near Savannah, Georgia.